Digger: Unearthing Life's Stories

By: Martin Thompson

Martin Thompson Books

Fort Worth, Texas

All rights reserved. No part of this publication may be reproduced, stored in a retrieval system, or transmitted in any form or by any means,

electronic, mechanical, photocopying, recording, or otherwise, except for brief quotations in reviews, educational works, or other uses permitted by copyright law.

Published in 2026 by

Martin Thompson Books

Hardcover ISBN: 979-8-9947796-5-1

Paperback ISBN: 979-8-9947796-4-4

E-ISBN: 979-8-9947796-6-8

Printed in the United States of America

No part of this publication may be used to train generative artificial intelligence (AI) models. The publisher and author reserve all rights related to the use of this content in machine learning.

All company and product names mentioned in this book may be trademarks or registered trademarks of their respective owners. They are used for identification purposes only and do not imply endorsement or affiliation.

Dedication

To Janice and Jon, to lifelong friends and their families

who made the journey sweeter,

to the incredible people I had the honor to work alongside,

and to the families who trusted me to serve them in their greatest times of need — Thank you. You've made this a life worth writing about.

Author's Note

This book began as a simple idea and quickly turned into something much larger.

For nearly five decades, I have worked in funeral service, a profession most people encounter only during life's hardest moments. Along the way, I've witnessed extraordinary grief, remarkable resilience, and more love than I ever imagined possible. I've also learned something that surprises people: even in the shadow of loss, humor has a way of showing up uninvited.

Sometimes it arrives like a nervous laugh.

Sometimes, it's an absurd moment that no one could have planned.

And sometimes, if you're paying attention, it shows up as a reminder that life insists on being lived—even on the hardest days.

Some readers may recognize pieces of these stories from an earlier book, Funeral Begins with Fun. Over time, I realized there were stories I hadn't told, moments I'd rushed past, and a voice that had been softened more than I intended. This book is my opportunity to return to those stories with a little more honesty, a little more humor, and a clearer sense of what I wanted to say in the first place. Some stories are familiar, others are new, and many have been reshaped—not to change their meaning, but to tell them more fully. In short, this is the book I was trying to write all along.

Digger: Unearthing Life's Stories is not a how-to book about funeral service, nor is it a collection of sermons or lessons. It is a gathering of moments—some funny, some tender, some uncomfortable, and many unforgettable. The stories here are rooted in real experiences, though names, details, and timelines have been adjusted at times to respect privacy and memory. The heart of each story, however, remains true.

I've tried to tell these stories the same way they were lived: honestly, imperfectly, and with a sense of humor that never forgets the humanity beneath it all. If you find yourself laughing in one chapter and quietly reflecting in the next, that's intentional. That's how life has always presented itself to me.

If you work in funeral service, I hope you recognize pieces of yourself in these lines. If you're reading as someone who has experienced loss—or inevitably will—I hope these stories remind you that grief and grace often walk hand in hand. And if you're simply here for the stories, then pull up a chair. You're welcome to this conversation.

Thank you for trusting me with your time. I hope what follows feels less like a book and more like a shared moment—one story at a time.

— Martin Thompson

Table of Contents

Dedication iv

Author's Note v

Chapter 1: Born on April Fool's Day 1

Chapter 2: Workers, Not Royalty 4

Chapter 3: The House Where Everyone Knew Your Business 8

Chapter 4: Learning Early What Death Looked Like 12

Chapter 5: Catholic School, Questionable Judgment 16

Chapter 6: Nicknames Stick for a Reason 21

Chapter 7: High School: Character Building (Whether I Wanted It or Not) 26

Chapter 8: Loose in Europe 30

Chapter 9: Teeny Weeny College and the Art of Balancing 37

Chapter 10: Cash, Caskets, and a Company Called Marcellus 41

Chapter 11: The Semester My Brain Clocked In 46

Chapter 12: Lordy, That Boy Graduated 51

Chapter 13: Two Cities, Two Schools, One Big Decision 56

Chapter 14: The Mortuary Student Nobody Expected 59

Chapter 15: Learning Death the Right Way 62

Interlude: A Very Quick History of Funeral Service 66

Chapter 16: The Night Shift Teaches You Everything 77

Chapter 17: Maybe Too Optimistic 82

Chapter 18: 1984: It's a Boy 90

Chapter 19: SL 500 93

Chapter 20: What Not to Say at a Funeral 95

Chapter 21: South Padre or Bust 98

Chapter 22: Can I Get a Haircut 101

Chapter 23: Cowboys, Charity, and a Very Satisfying Redemption 103

Chapter 24: From Fairway to Fleeing: The Great Club Switch of '88 107

Chapter 25: Some of the Best..................110

Chapter 26: April Fools and Divorce Blues..................113

Chapter 27: Honeymoon Surprises..................115

Chapter 28: Farm Life and Cosmic Consequences..................118

Chapter 29: Scouting Shenanigans..................121

Chapter 30: Funeral Home Adventures..................124

Chapter 31: Vic's Last Laugh..................128

Chapter 32: The Turning Point..................131

Chapter 33: From Tee Time to Funeral Home..................133

Chapter 34: From Remodel to Roll Call: The Grapevine Gamble 137

Chapter 35: Candice: The Worldly One..................140

Chapter 36: From Unknown to Unstoppable: Conquering Grapevine..................144

Chapter 37: From Joiner to Country Undertaker..................147

Chapter 38: Docking Dilemmas..................151

Chapter 39: Chapel Charades: From Dream to Dollhouse to Desperation..................155

Chapter 40: When Growth Looked Like the Answer..................158

Chapter 41: Keller Didn't Want a Funeral Home (Until It Did)...161

Chapter 42: The Slow Discovery of the Trap..................163

Chapter 43: A Profitable Partnership and a Pricey Problem..................166

Chapter 44: Back to Basics: Fort Worth or Bust..................170

Chapter 45: From Typewriters to Tech Titans..................173

Chapter 46: Funeral Moves & April Fools'..................177

Chapter 47: Renovation Odyssey 180

Chapter 48: Funeral Service in Pandemic Times 185

Chapter 49: Nobody Does This Alone 188

Chapter 50: Blood, Business, and the Funeral Home......................193

Chapter 51: Who Really Backed the Note..196

Chapter 52: Between Tee Times and Lifetimes.................................199

Chapter 53: Four A.M...202

Conclusion: Burying the Last Laugh 206

Acknowledgments 207

About the Author 209

Chapter 1: Born on April Fool's Day

I made my grand entrance into the world on April 1, 1958, a date best known for pranks, practical jokes, and people being fooled into believing things that probably shouldn't be believed. Fitting, really.

At exactly 5:26 a.m. in Fort Worth, Texas, I showed up first. My twin sister followed five minutes later, proving from the start that she was more efficient than I was. Together, we became the fifth and sixth children born to our parents, Guy and Kathleen Thompson, who were by then well acquainted with chaos.

When people start digging into their ancestry, they usually hope to discover something impressive—that they're descended from royalty, a war hero, a senator, or at the very least someone with a statue. I did a little digging myself and discovered... none of that.

On both sides of my family, we've always been workers.

Farmers. Wagon builders. Cattlemen. Ice cream store owners. Movers. Milkmen. Chicken farmers. Just regular folks who got up early, worked hard, and didn't make a habit of telling the world about it. No presidents. No senators. No high society. And honestly, I wouldn't trade that heritage for anything.

I've traced the Thompson family line back more than ten generations, and one thing is clear—we've been around a long time.

My dad, Guy Wilbur Thompson Jr., was born in Fort Worth to Guy Wilbur Thompson Sr., a man we all called Daddy Guy. He came to Texas from Muhlenberg, Kentucky, though for five generations before him, the Thompsons lived in Virginia. Go back even farther, and you'll find our earliest ancestors just south of Boston, which means, at some point, a distant relative of mine probably stood near Boston Harbor during the whole tea-tossing incident. Hopefully watching. Not participating.

From there, the Thompsons migrated south to Virginia, then west to Kentucky, and finally on to Texas, chasing better land, better weather, or just running from bad decisions.

One thing is certain: we loved recycling names. Every generation had a Richard, a John, and a William. Thankfully, we didn't recycle my grandfather's brothers' names: Thurston, Thexton, and Thesby Thompson.

Can you imagine being named Thesby?

I'd never have survived elementary school.

On my dad's mother's side, the Richardsons added their own chapter to the story. Eula Richardson Thompson—Nana to us—was a Weatherford farm girl with deep ranching roots. Her father was both a farmer and a cattle rancher, and unlike most people of his time, he wrote down his life story.

One of the more painful chapters involved his ranch in Cisco, Texas. After enduring a brutal two-year drought, he lost the land—only to see it later become part of the Cisco–Eastland Oil Boom of 1919. When someone asked him why he had left just before oil was discovered, he replied simply:

"A man never profits from land that another person leaves for greener pastures."

That's Texas wisdom in its purest form.

Here's the part that still amazes me: my grandmother's parents' original log cabin home now sits in the Log Cabin Village in Fort Worth. I lived here my entire life and didn't know that until I was in my sixties. Family history hiding in plain sight.

The Richardson migration followed a familiar Texas pattern—Massachusetts to Virginia, then Kentucky, Missouri, and finally Texas in the mid-1800s. No crowns. No marble halls. Just pioneers, ranchers, and business owners who helped build this part of the country one hard day at a time.

So that's half of where I come from.

A long line of hard workers. A few questionable naming decisions. And a birth date that practically guaranteed I wouldn't take myself too seriously.

Born into a family full of characters, on a day full of jokes.

From the very beginning, I was destined to have a story to tell.

Chapter 2: Workers, Not Royalty

My mother, Kathleen Marie Simon Thompson, made her way from the bustling metropolis of Toledo, Ohio, to what was then the not-so-bustling Fort Worth, Texas. Her parents, Victor Eugene Simon and Ursula Kelly Simon, were the quintessential Midwest couple—tough, hardworking, and the kind of people who could weather just about any storm, including an economic one.

Grampy, as we called him, ran a coal business in Ohio, supplying warmth to homes that experienced winter. (Unlike Texas, where we tend to act like the apocalypse is coming when the temperature drops below forty.) Eventually, oil rudely stepped in and put him out of business, forcing a career pivot before career pivots were fashionable.

I remember Grampy as the kind of guy who could watch a baseball game on television while listening to another one on the radio—multitasking before multitasking was cool. He and his brothers were apparently pretty good baseball players, with some even making it to the big leagues. But when the coal business collapsed, Grampy packed up and headed south to Texas, trading coal for oil-field supplies. A classic Texas reinvention story.

Grampy arrived in Fort Worth first, leaving Grammy and the kids back in Toledo to finish out the school year. He stayed at the Texas Hotel, but homesickness eventually set in. That's when he went to the Monsignor at St. Patrick's Cathedral and asked if he knew anyone with a room for rent.

And just like that, Grampy ended up renting from my dad.

At the time, Dad had recently bought a duplex, living on one side while his parents lived on the other. He and Grampy hit it off immediately, forming a friendship that would accidentally rewrite family history.

Here's the funny part.

When Grampy went back to Ohio for Christmas, he invited Dad to come along—with one very specific plan: introduce him to his daughter Terry.

Spoiler alert: that's not my mom.

After a few nights of partying with Terry, Dad decided he needed a break. So, who did he end up spending time with instead?

Her sister, Kathleen.

And just like that, instead of Guy and Terry, it became Guy and Kathleen.

Nice try, Grampy.

Grammy was a proud Irishwoman who had earned a college degree from Bowling Green University, which wasn't exactly common for women back then. Grampy, on the other hand, came from French ancestry. Thanks to the two of them, I ended up with a cocktail of Irish, French, English, and Scottish blood—or, as some might say, a mutt with a decent tolerance for whiskey and a love for good bread.

While Dad ran Harveson & Cole Funeral Home, Mom managed just about everything else—chauffeur, chef, teacher, referee, and all-around keeper of sanity for six kids. We weren't rolling in money, but we weren't scraping by either. What we lacked in luxury, we made up for in a strong Catholic upbringing, a crowded house, and a front-row seat at every mass and funeral we ever attended.

We even had a permanent pew at St. Mary's Catholic Church. Not because we were special—because we had no choice.

Some of my earliest memories are a little fuzzy, but a few stand out clearly: kindergarten at Mrs. Massey's, where I probably learned how to color inside the lines but not much else; a newspaper photo of me and my twin sister, Martha, on a seesaw at age three—the closest either of us ever came to child stardom; and my mother's elaborate Christmas card productions, which one year featured me playing Baby Jesus in a homemade nativity scene.

I peeked early.

But the real highlight of my childhood was our backyard.

We lived in a big two-story house with a wraparound porch, perfect for watching Texas thunderstorms roll in. My twin sister, Martha, and I were part of a six-kid circus—Cindy, Vic, Teacy, Tim, and us, the twins. Mom and Dad gave everyone creative pet names, except Martha and me. By the time they got to us, they'd run out of ideas, so we were stuck with our actual names.

That backyard is also where I unknowingly began my career in funeral service.

Any animal that met its demise within a six-block radius received the full backyard funeral treatment. Birds, squirrels, cats, you name it. The neighborhood kids would gather, and I'd lead the procession, a shoebox coffin in hand. We even had designated sections: one for squirrels, one for birds, one for cats, and a premium plot reserved for Poochie, our beloved dog.

Poochie was the only one who received a full-metal casket.

Funeral director foreshadowing? Absolutely.

Fast forward twenty-five years, my siblings and I took a nostalgic trip back to the old house. The new owners were nice folks, and we shared stories about our childhood adventures—like the time we discovered you could drain the bathtub from outside the bathroom, a prank that somehow never got old.

They loved hearing about our antics.

Right up until we mentioned the backyard cemetery.

When we casually explained that dozens of deceased animals were buried out back, their expressions changed noticeably.

One week later, the house went on the market.

Oops.

Some things, it turns out, are better left buried.

And that, folks, is how I got my start in the funeral business: shoebox caskets, processions of neighborhood kids, a backyard cemetery with proper sections, and an early instinct to make sure the deceased received a respectful send-off.

Who knew a childhood hobby would turn into a lifelong profession?

Buckle up. This ride is only just getting started.

Chapter 3: The House Where Everyone Knew Your Business

My education began at Mrs. Massey's Kindergarten School, where I was introduced to the thrilling world of the ABCs, 123s, and the fine art of coloring inside the lines. It was also where the early pattern of my life took shape: my twin sister excelled academically, and I... explored other areas of personal development.

While Martha sailed through lessons with ease and enthusiasm, I found myself focused on more pressing matters—like how to secure a girlfriend before the age of six. Success. I managed to woo a cute little blonde girl, whom I proudly considered my girlfriend. I may not have mastered reading yet, but I was an early adopter of charm.

That same year, I formed one of my first clear memories, and it wasn't about finger painting.

One early morning, my mother took us downtown Fort Worth to see President John F. Kennedy leaving the Hotel Texas after a breakfast event. If something involved the Church, nuns, or anything even vaguely Catholic, my mom was going to be front and center—and JFK was the ultimate Catholic icon. We watched him leave the Hotel, then headed home to get ready for school.

Not long after, my mother came in crying. She told us the President had been shot.

Even at five years old, I knew it was terrible, though I didn't fully understand its weight. For days, our television stayed glued to the coverage, and like the rest of the country, we watched the funeral—somber and unforgettable, even through the eyes of a kid who didn't fully know why he felt so quiet inside.

After my stellar performance at Mrs. Massey's (ahem), I was enrolled at St. Mary's Elementary School on Magnolia Street in Fort Worth. St. Mary's was run by nuns—and not the friendly, guitar-strumming kind you see in The Sound of Music. These nuns wore full-length black habits, stiff white wimples, and what I'm convinced were boots built for battle.

They looked serious. And trust me, they were.

To make things more interesting, the Thompson family was fully represented at St. Mary's. There was no escaping family oversight. Martha and I were in first grade. Tim is in third. Teacy fifth. Vic seventh. with Cindy in eighth. With siblings stationed in every corner of the building, getting away with anything was next to impossible.

And in our house, any disciplinary action at school meant an encore performance at home. So, I had twice the motivation to at least try to stay out of trouble.

I remember St. Mary's as a massive two-story building, with an enormous cafeteria and hall in the basement. Years later, when I visited again, it seemed much smaller. Maybe I had grown—or maybe my memories of Catholic school were just larger than life.

Being a twin comes with perks and pains, especially in a Catholic school environment.

The perk is you always have a built-in friend—or at least a reliable witness when you're being falsely accused.

The pain is that you can never escape comparisons.

Martha was a straight-A student. Martha was the teacher's pet. Martha sat quietly and listened.

Me? I was more of a free spirit, which is what you call it when you're not academically inclined, but you're very gifted at distracting everyone else.

The nuns had a radar for troublemakers, and I'm pretty sure I showed up on their screens on day one. A good knuckle-rap with a ruler was practically a daily occurrence. Deserved? Probably. But still.

Back in the sixties, there were no fancy diagnoses like ADD or ADHD. If you were smart, you were "gifted." If you struggled, you were "lazy." If you talked too much, you were "disruptive." Unfortunately, I seemed to fall into the last two categories.

From first grade on, school felt like it was written in hieroglyphics. Studying was a mystery. Reading was an impossible code. Test-taking might as well have been rocket science.

Multiple-choice tests became a game of chance, and I tried to crack the code or at least be strategic about it. In my mind, I would say let's try: A, B, A, D, D, C… ah, what the heck, another C. Was it effective? Not even a little. Did it make me feel like I had a system? Absolutely. And in my defense, a twenty-five percent shot at glory was better than nothing.

Despite my academic struggles, school wasn't all bad. I had great friends. I thrived in PE. And of course, I developed an early appreciation for the opposite sex.

But lunch? Lunch was a nightmare.

Picture a brown paper bag that had been reused so many times it had more holes than the bag. Inside was usually a sandwich that was mostly condiments: butter and mayonnaise drowning a wafer-thin slice of mystery meat. The two things I absolutely despised were butter and mayo.

Mom's rule was simple: "This isn't a restaurant; you'll eat what you're served."

I did what any starving kid with standards would do. Into the trash the sandwich went, and I survived on chips and chocolate milk—basically the official diet of Catholic school survival.

Between tragic lunches and dinners that weren't much better, I managed to graduate high school weighing a whopping 130 pounds. For context, some ninth graders today weigh more than that. But who needs extra padding when you've got charm, right?

Looking back, Catholic school was a character-building experience. It taught discipline. It kept me humble. And it made sure I developed a healthy respect for nuns, rulers, and cafeteria mysteries.

And as for the academic struggles, let's just say I eventually figured things out—just not without a few more detours along the way.

Chapter 4: Learning Early What Death Looked Like

Some people come into your life for a season. Others change the direction of your life forever.

I was lucky enough to meet a few of those people early on—and I've never stopped being grateful for them.

Starting in first grade, I had good friends, but one stood out from the beginning: Jimmy Suarez.

Jimmy was the kind of friend everyone hopes for:

He always saved me a seat.

He always picked me first for his team.

And he always shared his lunch, which, given my tragic sandwich situation, made him nothing short of heroic.

But as important as Jimmy was to me, the real turning point in my life came from his dad.

Jimmy's dad was everyone's second dad—the kind of man who always had time for kids who weren't even his own. My own father was a master of funeral service, but camping trips, sports, and outdoor adventures weren't exactly his arena. Jimmy's dad, on the other hand, filled that gap without ever making a big deal about it.

He was my first baseball coach.

He took me camping with their family.

And most importantly, he introduced me to the game of golf.

That last one changed everything.

I was about ten years old when Jimmy told me, "We're going to play golf with my dad." I had no idea what golf even was. We headed to a little nine-hole course called Sycamore, and I stood there gripping a club for the first time, not knowing which end was supposed to hit the ball.

There were a few whiffs.

A few topped shots.

And then—somehow—I connected.

The ball took off. It probably traveled fifty yards, maybe less. But to me, it might as well have been a Tiger Woods drive down the middle of Augusta. I was instantly, completely hooked.

From that day on, golfing with Jimmy and his dad became a regular thing. Before long, Jimmy's dad handed me my first set of clubs:

A 3, 5, 7, and 9 iron

A 3-wood

A putter

And a handful of well-used range balls

They didn't match. They weren't shiny. But to me, they were priceless.

To this day, I can honestly say I can't thank anyone more for giving me something I love than Jimmy's dad. While my father was perfecting the art of a flawless funeral, Jimmy's dad was quietly shaping my golf swing—and, without knowing it, shaping a big part of who I would become. If it weren't for him, I'd probably be telling stories about my professional kickball career.

In fourth grade, life shifted again. My parents moved us to the west side of Fort Worth, which meant a new parish, a new school, and saying goodbye to Jimmy. I didn't know it at the time, but that move would introduce me to another lifelong friend.

Enter Holy Family Catholic School—and Griffin Gunter.

Griff was legendary for one thing: his backyard fort. This wasn't some flimsy plywood operation. It was a masterpiece. Think Swiss Family Robinson meets two kids with unlimited free time.

Griff's parents were just as legendary.

Mrs. G's lunches were on an entirely different level. Fast-forward to today: she is about to turn 102 and is still kind and as sharp as a whip.

Mr. G's backyard was the ultimate kids' paradise and the kind of man who stayed that way your whole life — steady, kind, and quietly present. I didn't know it then, but he'd end up being one of those people you never really stop missing.

As we got older, bikes became our freedom. We rode everywhere. We explored neighborhoods far beyond where we were supposed to go. If two wheels could get us there, we went.

One day in eighth grade, Griff and I took a long ride that ended near Z Boaz Golf Course. Out of nowhere, I was hit with the worst stomach pain I'd ever experienced. I collapsed. I couldn't ride. I couldn't even sit upright.

Without hesitation, Griff pushed both bikes all the way back to my house—several miles—while I barely held myself together. That's the kind of friend he was then and still is today, and we still play golf regularly.

At home, my mom took over. And in the Thompson household, being sick came with a very specific fear. You didn't exaggerate illness— you tried desperately to convince Mom you were fine. Why? Because her cure-all for just about everything involved an enema. I would have preferred almost any alternative.

This time, though, I couldn't fake it.

The next day, I was at the doctors.

Diagnosis: appendicitis.

Solution: emergency surgery.

And because my life seemed to follow a very specific pattern, I had the operation at St. Joseph's Hospital—run by nuns, of course.

Was appendicitis major surgery? Some people might say no. I say any surgery performed on me qualifies as major.

Griff had saved the day. If he hadn't got me home when he did, things could have turned out very differently.

By then, we had a whole crew of friends, and our childhood mischief was exactly what you'd expect:

BB guns fired from the fort (aiming optional)

Houses papered during slumber parties.

Bike jumps built in the woods near Ridgmar.

And the accidental discovery of a friend's dad's Playboy collection (purely for the articles, obviously)

We didn't know it yet, but those years were closing fast. Something bigger was coming—more structure, more responsibility, and fewer forts.

But golf had already found its way into my life.

Friendship had anchored me.

And the lessons I didn't know I was learning had already begun.

Chapter 5: Catholic School, Questionable Judgment

By the time I turned twelve, my life started filling up with uniforms.

School uniform. Scout uniform. And—because my mother never met an activity she couldn't sign me up for—choir uniform.

Each one came with rules. And each one came with adults who took those rules as if they were carved in stone tablets.

Scouting came first.

My brothers had already set the bar. Vic made it to Life Scout… and then discovered girls, a merit badge that Troop 32 did not offer. Tim, on the other hand, went all the way to Eagle Scout—quietly, efficiently, like he'd been born holding a compass.

So naturally, here I came.

I started out as a Webelo—basically a kid stuck in scouting purgatory: too old for Cub Scouts, not quite a Boy Scout, and still trying to figure out why we were tying knots when nobody in Fort Worth had ever needed a knot in real life.

By fourth grade, I earned my Arrow of Light, which sounds like something you win in a medieval tournament, and by fifth grade, I crossed over into Boy Scouts and joined Troop 32.

Troop 32 wasn't just a troop. Troop 32 was… a reputation.

We were sponsored by the Knights of Columbus and met downtown, behind their hall, in a little scout building I remember as small, which meant it was probably the size of a broom closet. But we didn't care. Because running the show was Ole Man Gillespie.

Ole Man wasn't just a scoutmaster. Ole Man was an institution.

He'd been doing scouting for over forty years, which meant he'd seen every excuse, every shortcut, and every "my dog ate my merit badge worksheet" story ever invented.

When we showed up at campouts with other troops, we walked around like we were somebody—because people knew Troop 32, and people definitely knew Ole Man. He expected a lot, and somehow… we did it.

This was not a troop built on sing-alongs and roasted marshmallows.

Troop 32 was an Eagle Scout machine.

Every campout had a purpose: earn a merit badge, advance a rank, learn something useful. Tenderfoot, Second Class, First Class, Star, Life, Eagle—Ole Man had a plan, and we were in it. Even after you made Eagle, the pressure didn't stop. Then came Palms—Bronze, Silver, Gold—because apparently sleeping in the woods wasn't enough. We needed homework too.

We even had our own campground, Camp Murrin, down in an area perfectly named Whiskey Flats. Camp Murrin ran alongside a creek where we pitched our tents, and by Sunday afternoon, I would be less "boy" and more "mosquito bite collection," loosely held together by determination and Off! repellent.

Now here's something I didn't appreciate until I got older:

We scouts were "roughing it" in one area… and Ole Man and the leaders were roughing it in another area that suspiciously included cases of beer, better food, and things like sardines and pickled pig's feet.

Let me be clear: I am not counting sardines and pickled pigs' feet in the "better food" category. That's just punishment with salt.

But nothing kept me away from campouts.

Being a Catholic troop meant we also had Catholic retreat campouts and big multi-troop events—Jamborees. And at one of those Jamborees, the thing every scout wanted happened: Order of the Arrow.

They held the Tap-Out ceremony. We all stood in a long line facing forward while the Brotherhood came up behind us. You didn't turn around. You didn't flinch. You just stood there trying to act like your heart wasn't pounding out of your chest.

And if you got chosen, they'd grab your shoulders and tap you out:

Three long taps on your left shoulder.

One long and two quick taps on your right.

When I got tapped out, I'm telling you, I felt like royalty.

Of course, the Tap-Out was just the invitation. The real work came later, finishing the obligations and earning your place. But still… for a kid like me, that moment was everything.

Summer camp was the crown jewel.

We had two options: Camp Leonard near Granbury and Worth Ranch near Palo Pinto. My first year was Camp Leonard—great camp, great memories.

But Worth Ranch? Worth Ranch was Mecca.

We had our own campsite there as well—Ole Man Campsite—right across from the archery range. Everything was a hike: chow hall, pool, and especially the river stuff—canoeing, sailing, even water skiing. That river felt like freedom.

And during downtime, we went rattlesnake hunting—because apparently that was considered a reasonable recreational activity in Texas.

By the end of the week, we had over twenty rattlesnakes hanging around camp like trophies. At night we'd sit around the fire, tell stories, and feel invincible—like life was always going to be campfires and friends and a sky full of stars.

Being the youngest in the family had one downside: I inherited everything.

My sleeping bag was thin enough to qualify as a napkin.

My tent had more duct tape than fabric.

My flashlight barely lit up my own hand.

But you make do.

And scouting gave me something else: lifelong friends.

One of the best was Chris Guinn. Chris was that guy.

He always had the best gear: a brand-new uniform, shiny boots, everything pressed as if he were headed for a job interview instead of the woods. He had great hair. And the girls noticed him early, which is how you knew he was dangerous.

But the real reason I loved camping with Chris was simple:

Chris had an ice chest.

And Chris's ice chest was like the luxury suite of summer camp.

Now the camp food wasn't terrible—better than some of my childhood meals—but Chris's ice chest was on another level: lunch meat, candy... and one time, way down in the bottom, two bottles of wine.

We had no idea what to do with it but figured it out. And stared at it like we'd uncovered contraband from the Vatican.

Looking back, all my closest friends seemed to have two things in common:

good hearts

better food than I had

So maybe I was just perpetually starving.

In 1972, six of us stood at our Court of Honor and earned the rank of Eagle Scout—including Chris and Phil Shaw, who later married my twin. That's still one of the proudest moments of my life. Scouting taught me leadership, patience, teamwork, and how to finish what you start—lessons that followed me long after the uniforms were folded up and the tents got retired.

And right about the time I was learning to lead...

My life took another unexpected turn.

One afternoon, my mom said casually, "Get in the car. We're running an errand."

That is never a sentence you want to hear in the Thompson household, because "errand" could mean groceries… or it could mean you're about to be signed into something that requires a uniform.

Destination: Texas Boys Choir Headquarters.

Purpose: Apparently, I was about to become a choir boy.

Before I could process what was happening, somebody called my name and told me to sing the National Anthem. I sang. Then they clapped the rhythm and told me to clap it back.

A few minutes later: "Congratulations—you're in."

In what?!

Suddenly, I had daily practice, weekend rehearsals, and discipline that made Catholic school nuns look relaxed. The choir ran on precision and obedience. You showed up. You did what you were told. You didn't question much.

Until I did.

One week, my parents left town. I skipped practice. Completely. When they got back, my mom and the choir director showed up at Holy Family and pulled me out of class.

"If you apologize," Mom said, "you can stay in the choir."

For the first time in my life, I looked my mother straight in the eye and said, "No."

It wasn't a rebellion. It wasn't anger. It was clarity.

Scouting taught me how to lead.

Choir taught me how to follow.

And somewhere in between… I learned how to decide for myself.

Chapter 6: Nicknames Stick for a Reason

By the time I was thirteen, I had figured out two important things about life:

I liked having money.

And nobody was particularly interested in giving it to me.

So, like any motivated kid with ambition and a questionable sense of leverage, I went looking for work.

My first real job came courtesy of the Catholic Church - an institution known for many things, but not for generous hourly wages.

Holy Family had just completed a new school building, and somebody donated enough money to build a "new playground." But this wasn't your classic playground with grass and swings and a metal slide hot enough to brand your thighs.

This was more like an abstract art installation.

Winding concrete sidewalks. Strange equipment. Gravel everywhere.

And weeds. Lots of weeds. The weeds loved it. The weeds were thriving.

Monsignor Wolf hired me to weed it.

Pay rate: $1 per hour.

Texas summers, for the record, are about as forgiving as a nun with a ruler. I started early, worked until noon, then wandered over to the rectory to see if there was anything else I could do - because I was thirteen and still believed hard work automatically led to payment.

Each week, I'd tell Monsignor how many hours I worked - twenty-five, thirty, whatever it was.

And each week he would say the same thing:

"Keep track of your hours."

What I eventually learned was that this translated loosely to:

"I'll pay you later."

"Maybe."

"If I remember."

By the end of summer, I had close to 300 hours logged and was already mentally spending my three hundred dollars. That was real money in my thirteen-year-old brain.

Finally, the day came.

Monsignor reached into the collection basket, pulled out five rolls of quarters, and handed them to me.

"Here you go, Martin. I bet you've never seen this much money," he said, with a pat on the head.

I stood there holding those quarters, doing the math.

This wasn't three hundred dollars.

This was fifty.

Now, you don't argue with priests - especially when you're standing there holding their quarters. I thanked him politely, walked out, and learned something that would come in handy later in life:

Get paid up front.

Naturally, I took my "fortune" straight to a convenience store and blew it on several buckets of gum, because nothing says "financial wisdom" like investing in chewy sugar.

After my brief career in ecclesiastical landscaping, I decided I needed a better system - one where money was at least theoretically guaranteed.

Enter: the paper route.

I signed up with The Fort Worth Press, an afternoon paper with no Saturday edition and a Sunday morning newspaper roughly the size and weight of a small appliance. My route ran from Camp Bowie down to I-

30, and from Hulen over to Merrick - plus a few apartment complexes that felt like they were designed by people who hated paperboys.

Monday through Friday wasn't bad. I'd bike to the paper drop, roll eighty to a hundred papers, and start tossing them on porches.

Sunday mornings were another beast entirely.

Over one hundred twenty-five papers.

Two drop locations.

And every one of those Sunday papers was thick enough to stop a bullet.

That oversized paper bag felt like hauling a refrigerator across Fort Worth.

I did what any smart kid would do. I hired help.

I recruited my neighborhood buddies with the most powerful currency known to middle-school boys:

Dunkin' Donuts hot chocolate and cream-filled donuts on Sunday mornings.

It worked.

Every Sunday morning, before the sun came up, we'd roam the streets like a sugar-fueled gang. Was it night? Was it morning? Nobody knew. We tossed papers, inhaled donuts, and felt like we were getting away with something just because the adults were asleep.

If they helped during the week, I'd pay them in root beer floats at Mobley's Ridglea - the kind in frosty mugs that made you feel rich even if you weren't.

The houses paid like clockwork.

The apartment people, on the other hand, were elusive.

They wouldn't answer the door.

They claimed they never ordered the paper.

Or they'd hit me with, "Come back next week."

Meanwhile, I had already paid for every paper I delivered.

That's when I learned the part of business nobody puts on a motivational poster:

Collections will make you hate people.

About the time my enthusiasm started fading - and my profits started looking suspiciously like Monsignor's quarter math - another opportunity showed up. One that combined two things I loved: golf and money.

My brother had joined Shady Oaks Country Club, and I'd caddied for him a few times. Hanging around the club, I noticed boys my age working as bag boys. They have to be around golf all day. They made actual money. And, most importantly, they got tips.

I applied. Art Hall, the golf pro, hired me.

Pay rate: one dollar and twenty-five cents an hour, plus tips.

I didn't even know what tips were. Once I found out, I decided I was a big fan of this whole "tip" concept.

The job was basically organized chaos. You ran carts, hauled bags, cleaned clubs, swapped morning bags for afternoon bags, and tried to look busy whenever somebody important was nearby.

And then there was Ben Hogan.

Mr. Hogan practiced at Shady Oaks a few times a week. When his Cadillac pulled in, whoever was closest to the bag room door got the call to shag balls.

I learned to recognize that car immediately.

And I learned to be "accidentally" near the door at exactly the right times.

He'd dump his shag bag of balls, tell you where to stand, and start with an eight iron. One by one, he hit shots that landed right at your feet. Not near your feet. At your feet.

You'd catch the ball on the first bounce in a towel, let it spin itself clean, and drop it back in the bag. Then he'd motion you back as he changed clubs.

It didn't matter what iron he pulled - the ball kept landing at your feet like it had a reservation.

When he moved into his woods, those came in hotter. I learned to catch those on the second bounce if I wanted to keep all my fingers. If you missed one, you didn't chase it. You just made a mental note and picked it up later - quietly - with your dignity.

When he finished, he'd putt a few out, you'd gather everything up, and that was that.

Then he'd hand you a crisp five-dollar bill.

That was serious money for a thirteen-year-old.

I worked at Shady Oaks until I was eighteen, and to this day, it remains one of the best jobs I have ever had. It paid me, fed my golf addiction, and taught me something important up close:

Excellence isn't accidental.

It's practiced.

Over and over.

Right at your feet.

And somewhere between a priest's quarters, a Sunday paper bag, and Ben Hogan's eight iron, I was getting an education nobody at school was offering.

I was still skinny.

Still figuring it out.

But I was moving forward.

And high school was waiting.

Chapter 7: High School: Character Building (Whether I Wanted It or Not)

High school at Nolan Catholic felt like the beginning of real life. Not adulthood exactly—but something close enough to taste. There were football games, basketball rivalries, dances, friendships that suddenly mattered more than they probably should have, and a steady stream of opportunities to get myself into trouble. It was louder, faster, and far less forgiving than grade school—and I loved every minute of it.

But if I'm honest, there was one thing that pulled everything else into orbit.

. Golf.

Jimmy's dad had unknowingly changed the direction of my life years earlier by putting a club in my hands, and Shady Oaks had taken that spark and poured gasoline on it. By the time I reached Nolan, golf wasn't just something I liked; it was something I planned for around. I was already a bag boy, already chasing tips, already positioning myself near the bag room door in hopes of shagging balls for Ben Hogan like it was an Olympic tryout. When I found out Nolan had a golf team, it wasn't a casual decision.

I didn't just join.

I moved in mentally. Put me in, Coach.

Nolan, like every Catholic institution I'd attended before it, had rules. Lots of them. But this was a different upgrade. I'd come up under nuns armed with rulers, and by then I was practically immune. Bring it on, Sister. Nolan, however, introduced a new level of discipline: Brothers. These weren't the warm, pat-you-on-the-head-after-Mass types. These were serious men with serious expressions and fiberglass paddles that meant business. And high school, as it turns out, provides plenty of opportunities to test the limits of authority.

The school prides itself on being forward-thinking, which is how we ended up with something called the Mod schedule. Classes were broken into twenty-minute blocks, strung together in combinations that felt advanced and confusing at the same time. Between Mods, we were given "free time," which was meant to be spent studying in the library or working quietly in a lab.

In practice, it became a master class in avoiding supervision.

The Student Center, the parking lot, and any unsupervised corner of campus became popular destinations. Nolan even had designated smoking areas—yes, smoking areas—with parental permission. Mine worked beautifully until the administration noticed that my mother's signature looked suspiciously like my own handwriting.

Lesson learned: if you're going to forge a signature, don't sign it exactly the way you sign your name.

Chris Guinn and I figured out early that if you were going to survive Nolan—and maybe even enjoy it—you needed to stay one step ahead. We somehow ended up in charge of lining up bands for school dances, which meant going into nightclubs before we were even legally allowed in. We were "scouting talent," which sounded official enough to get us through the door. Occasionally, we were even allowed to sample the beer purely for research.

There was one non-negotiable requirement for any band we booked: they had to play Stairway to Heaven.

That was for me. I wanted to dance with my girlfriend to that song—at least until it hit the second half, when dancing became impossible and everyone just kind of stood there wondering what to do with their arms. It didn't matter. That song meant something, and if a band couldn't pull it off, they weren't playing our dance.

For those of us on the golf team, the Mod schedule was nothing short of divine intervention. We learned quickly how to stack classes early in the day, freeing ourselves by late morning. By eleven or twelve, we were done—free to head to the golf course as if it were a required extension of our education.

And we did. Every day.

My golf crew became some of my closest friends—Mike Hood, a fellow Eagle Scout; the Berkoski brothers; Phil Shaw, another Eagle who would eventually marry my twin; and a handful of other guys who understood two things very well: how to smoke without getting caught, and how to enjoy an afternoon. We weren't sneaking off; we were living. Golf, cigarettes, laughter, and wide-open afternoons. I wasn't anywhere near the top of the team, but I was exactly where I wanted to be.

That illusion took a hit during my freshman year at my first real golf tournament.

I was one of the first to tee off, standing on the box in front of what felt like a stadium full of people. I settled in, took a deep breath, and swung.

The ball went straight into a metal trash can about ten feet off the tee box.

The sound echoed.

Then the ball ricocheted—directly back behind me—into the crowd.

There are few walks lonelier than the one you take off a tee box after something like that.

Golf has a way of humbling you early, and often.

School wasn't the only place Nolan tested us. One year, our Ecology class took a trip to Big Bend, starting the day after Christmas. We were supposed to be back by December 31. Instead, a winter storm dumped several feet of snow, closed the pass out, and stranded us in our tents until January 1.

It was freezing. Miserable. The coldest few days of my life.

And I wouldn't trade it for anything.

Chris Guinn—my Eagle Scout tent mate years earlier—was there too. He was a constant through high school, through scouts, through the good decisions and the questionable ones. Somewhere along the way, I also dropped the nickname "Marty." That happened after my first girlfriend showed up with a homecoming mum that read Marty & Marti.

I decided right then I'd be Martin. Years later, "Digger" would take over, but that came much later.

Somehow, through all of this, I graduated high school without ever earning a single paddling. Considering my natural talent for mischief, I consider that a personal triumph. I wasn't lighting up the honor roll, but I was learning things that mattered—how to manage time just well enough, how to stay off the radar, how to avoid the wrath of fiberglass paddles, and how to find the people and places that made life feel right.

Looking back now, I have fond memories of Nolan—the teachers, the Nuns, the Brothers, the structure, and even the discipline. And in one of life's stranger full-circle moments, I've had the privilege of burying some of those same people in the years since.

A Catholic school never really lets you go.

It just follows you… politely… all the way to the cemetery.

High school didn't define where I was going, but it sharpened how I moved through the world. I learned what mattered to me. I learned what I didn't. And without realizing it at the time, I was being quietly prepared for something bigger than golf scores, Mod schedules, or graduation quotes.

Because while I thought the party might be winding down, it wasn't ending at all.

It was just getting ready to leave town.

And not long after Nolan loosened its grip, someone handed us passports, pointed us toward an airplane, and trusted a handful of Catholic-school survivors to represent Fort Worth somewhere over the Atlantic.

What could possibly go wrong?

Chapter 8: Loose in Europe

A wild European school trip, with lessons in culture, language, and underage… everything.

If Nolan taught me anything, it was that a Catholic school can offer two things at once: structure and loopholes. You could be sitting in a classroom one minute, "studying," and the next minute you were in the Student Center discussing the important issues of the day—like whether you could get out of fourth period if your coach needed you, or how long you could stand in a "designated smoking area" before a Brother appeared like Batman with a fiberglass paddle.

So, when the chance came for a pre-graduation trip to Europe, I didn't see it as a school trip.

I saw it as an opportunity to take my Nolan survival skills international.

There were thirteen high school kids, temporarily turned loose on the world—chaperoned by two young teachers I'll call Miss H and Miss A. They were freshly minted, energetic, and still at that point in their careers where they believed rules were flexible if the students were "learning." Bless them. They had no idea what they were about to supervise.

We left DFW like we were invading Normandy—loud, excited, and already acting like we'd been overseas for years. The plan was simple: fly to New York, connect to Paris, and start the European portion of our "educational experience."

The problem was… our plane had made an unexpected detour to Vietnam the night before.

Which is not a sentence you expect to hear when you're seventeen and wearing a Nolan jacket.

We sat in New York, waiting on a replacement plane, killing time and pretending we were seasoned travelers. We weren't. We were teenagers with matching luggage tags and the attention span of a gnat in a candy store.

Eventually, the replacement plane arrived. We boarded. And the moment we hit international airspace; the trip took on a tone that can only be described as: European studies with a minor in bad decisions.

Because somewhere over the Atlantic, two things became clear:

We were headed to places our parents had only seen in books.

Nobody on that plane was going to stop us from ordering whatever the drink menu offered.

Now, I'm not saying Miss H and Miss A encouraged it.

I'm just saying they didn't exactly tackle anyone in the aisle.

And at that moment, international airspace felt like a magical zone where the laws of Fort Worth didn't apply.

Flying with Jethro Tull (and annoying them for miles)

About the time we were settling into our new identity as "world travelers," we found out we weren't the only notable passengers.

Ian Anderson and the Jethro Tull band were on the same flight.

Yes. That Ian Anderson. That Jethro Tull.

I can only imagine their management team's reaction when they realized they'd been seated in the middle of a plane full of high school kids who had the boldness of youth and the persistence of door-to-door vacuum cleaner salesmen.

Autographs. Questions. "Are y'all really Jethro Tull?"

(As if someone would pretend to be Jethro Tull on a random flight to Paris.)

They were polite. We were relentless. It was a beautiful collision of rock stardom and teenage audacity.

Paris: museums, cathedrals, and my personal devotion to Star beer

We landed in Paris at the crack of dawn, checked into the Orly Hilton, splashed water on our faces, and immediately began what our itinerary called "cultural immersion."

Which means we ran through museums and cathedrals at full speed while pretending to absorb history.

We were teenagers. Our attention spans were short. Our energy was high. And if a building had been standing since the 1200s, we admired it for about eight seconds before asking where the nearest bar was.

That night, we took a barge cruise through Paris, the kind of thing that looks elegant on postcards and feels even more elegant when you're sitting at a table covered in empty bottles of a beer called Star.

No drinking age. No problem.

I don't remember the flavor profile. I remember the feeling—Paris glowing, the river moving, the city looking like it had been designed specifically to make a seventeen-year-old believe his life was turning into a movie.

Easter Sunday brought us to Mass at Notre Dame Cathedral—an awe-inspiring moment even for a kid who'd spent his life in Catholic churches. Notre Dame wasn't just a church; it was a cathedral that seemed to hold the weight of centuries. You could feel it in the air.

The only thing that broke the spell was the steady stream of nuns soliciting donations with the determination of a fundraiser trying to win a prize.

I clutched my money as if it were life support. Not because I wasn't generous, but because my budget had already been allocated to the essentials of European travel:

Beer and cigarettes.

Brussels and Amsterdam: Happy 17th birthday to me

From Paris, we moved on to Brussels, and then to Amsterdam—where I turned seventeen.

My parents had given Miss H and Miss A some cash for a birthday celebration. I'm sure they had pictured a nice dinner. A cake. Maybe a thoughtful, happy birthday song.

What they got instead was a bar. Slot machines. And an atmosphere that made it clear Europe had a very different definition of "age appropriate."

We went looking for a birthday spot and ended up in a place where Griff and I quickly realized something was… off. We were the only "guys," surrounded by women who, on closer inspection, were not exactly women.

We executed a retreat so fast it should've come with theme music.

We found another bar—dimly lit, full of Heineken, loud in that wonderful European way where nobody seems to care if you're laughing too much. And it was going beautifully until we noticed a steady stream of men heading through a door in the back… and never coming back out.

One of our crew took a picture—because high school boys will document their own demise like it's a hobby—and we were thrown out so fast I'm surprised we didn't leave skid marks.

Turns out, we wandered into a brothel.

Oops.

That's how I celebrated seventeen: accidentally, loudly, and with a story my mother would've preferred I never had.

Rotterdam: tulips, cheese, and the night the English Channel fought back.

Next stop: Rotterdam.

Two things stood out:

Tulip fields as far as the eye could see—like God decided to paint the earth with a box of crayons.

The best cheese I had ever tasted in my life.

I bought a massive block of it because when you're seventeen and in Europe, you make decisions based on emotion, not policy.

I did not realize food wasn't allowed on the cruise ship we were about to take across the English Channel.

So, there we were, standing near the ship, eating cheese like starving peasants who'd just robbed a dairy.

It felt responsible at the time.

It was not.

Because that night, on a rocking ship, with my stomach full of questionable amounts of cheese, I discovered a brand-new European landmark:

The bathroom.

I saw it so many times it started to feel like home.

Let's just say the ship was rocking… and so was I.

London: English that wasn't English, and the moment the trip turned real.

Finally, we arrived in London and checked into the Victoriaville Station Hotel.

It was a relief to hear English again—until we asked a Londoner for directions to Westminster Abbey.

He responded with pure gibberish.

We stood there nodding politely, pretending we understood every word, while comprehending absolutely nothing.

It reminded me of the time one of the girls in our group tried to ask for a bathroom in French in Paris and ended up requesting a "room with a bath."

Lost in translation is real. And it's humiliating.

But London was also where the trip became more than beer and stories. We did see the sights—history you could touch, buildings older than anything back home, and the kind of atmosphere that makes you realize the world is bigger than your neighborhood, your school, your plans.

And for Griff and me, there was another highlight: seeing the original production of Jesus Christ Superstar in London.

That show hit me in a way I didn't expect. I'd grown up Catholic, surrounded by rules and rituals, and there was something about seeing faith, doubt, and humanity put on stage that made it feel… real. Not tidy. Not sanitized. Real.

I didn't know it then, but that sense of life being both messy and holy would become a theme. We tried to get tickets to see Tommy, but we didn't succeed.

I met a cute girl from Elkin, NC, and decided she would become my girlfriend for life, but life is tough from Ft Worth to Elkin.

Graduation: "The party's over."

Then we came home.

And suddenly it was graduation day.

We were asked to write something heartfelt for the yearbook. Something inspiring. Something about our bright future.

Most people wrote what you'd expect:

"Thanks to my teachers."

"Never stop learning."

"The best is yet to come."

Me?

I wrote: "The party's over."

My mother was not impressed.

But in my defense, it felt honest. Not sad—just honest. I'd had fun. I'd survived the paddles and the Mods and the Catholic-school circus.

I'd been to Europe. I'd turned seventeen in a way that probably shaved a year off my mother's lifespan. And now the music was fading out.

And here's the thing I didn't realize yet:

The party wasn't over.

It was just changing locations.

Because not long after that—January 1st, 1976, at 9:10 p.m.—Dad walked into the den with the kind of calm expression that meant he'd already made the decision.

"You've been itching to work at the funeral home," he said.

"Well… I've got a job for you."

And just like that, the next chapter of my life started—quietly, unexpectedly, and with the faint feeling that I was stepping into something that would follow me forever.

Chapter 9: Teeny Weeny College and the Art of Balancing

Texas Wesleyan was affectionately known as Teeny Weeny College, and it earned the nickname honestly. You couldn't hide there. You couldn't disappear into the back row. If you skipped class, someone noticed—usually a professor, sometimes another student, occasionally both. It was the kind of place where people knew your name, your major, and whether you were bluffing your way through a discussion.

Which, for the record, I did more than once.

My days quickly settled into a rhythm that looked exhausting on paper but somehow worked in real life.

School in the morning.

Work in the afternoon.

The funeral home at night—every other night, without fail.

In between all of that, I tried to pass as a normal college student.

After classes, I headed to L. O. Hammons, selling clothes to people who somehow trusted a college kid to dress them for work, weddings, and life events I hadn't experienced yet. It taught me how to talk to people, how to listen, and how to read room skills I didn't realize I was collecting but would rely on for the rest of my life.

Working at L. O. Hammons also taught me something else: if you're willing to ask, doors open. I used my dad's connections and started taking clothes directly to doctors, lawyers, and business owners—guys who didn't have time to shop but appreciated someone showing up with options. I'd bring a couple of suits, sport coats, and slacks, let them feel good about buying just one or two pieces, then take everything back for alterations. When I delivered the finished clothes, I never showed up empty-handed. Shirts, ties, socks, shoes—things that complemented what they'd already bought. It wasn't pushy. It was a service. And it worked.

I made good money on commission. Of course, I spent most of it on myself. By my last year at Wesleyan, I was wearing tailor-made clothes, showing up to class in a coat and tie, and carrying myself as if I belonged there. I was probably the best-dressed senior on campus, which sounds impressive until you know I also had a hefty bill waiting for me at L. O. Hammons. That was after my cost-plus-ten-percent employee discount. Apparently, confidence is expensive.

Then there were the nights.

At Harveson & Cole, nothing changed just because I was in college. Phones still had to be answered on the second ring. The building still had to be walked. The quiet still demanded respect. I learned how to move from the noise of campus straight into the stillness of the funeral home without dragging one world into the other.

Sleep was optional.

Cokes were mandatory.

Somewhere in the middle of all that, I joined a fraternity. On paper, which sounds irresponsible. My fraternity brothers were some of the hardest-working people I knew. We studied late. We helped each other survive exams. And when our study sessions took place in a funeral home, nobody flinched.

Coffins in the background? Fine.

Phones ringing? Whatever.

We adjusted.

Funeral homes have a way of clarifying priorities.

And then there was Henry.

Henry was my sheepdog, and if you've ever had a dog arrive at exactly the right moment in your life, you understand. Henry wasn't just a pet—he was an anchor. When the schedule got heavy, when the nights ran long, when I started questioning whether I was stretching too thin, Henry was there. Always ready for a walk. Always present. Always reminding me that no matter how complicated life felt, some things were still simple.

He grounded me in ways I didn't fully appreciate until much later.

I had a steady girlfriend then, too. Not a distraction—a constant. Someone who knew the version of me juggling school, work, and responsibility and still believed I was headed somewhere. I didn't know exactly where yet, but I knew I wasn't drifting anymore.

Golf never left my life, either—but it changed.

Shady Oaks was behind me. Country clubs were for later chapters. During college, golf lived at municipal courses—where nobody cared who you were, what your GPA was, or how tired you looked. It was where time slowed just enough to breathe. I wasn't great. I never pretended to be. But I loved the rhythm of it, the quiet between shots, the way it cleared your head without asking questions.

Golf taught me patience long before I knew I'd need it.

Academically, something unexpected started to happen.

For most of my life, school has felt like a fight. I read slower than everyone else. I struggled to retain what I'd just read. Tests felt like traps designed by people whose brains worked differently from mine. Back then, nobody talked about ADD, ADHD, or learning differences. You weren't diagnosed—you were labeled.

Lazy.

Unfocused.

Not trying hard enough.

Somewhere in college, things began to shift.

I don't know exactly when it happened. I just know that quietly—almost without permission—reading started to make sense. Concepts stuck. For the first time, I wasn't just surviving classes. I understood them. It wasn't sudden. It wasn't dramatic.

But it was real.

Between classes, shifts at Hammons, nights at the funeral home, fraternity obligations, and whatever passed for a social life, I learned how to move between worlds. One moment, I'd be talking about marketing in a classroom. Next, I'd answer a phone call about arrangements, speaking softly, carefully, and respectfully.

It wasn't a switch I flipped.

It was a posture I adopted.

There were moments when exhaustion caught up with me. Nights when I wondered if the counselor's statistics might still win. Days when I questioned whether I'd taken on too much. But every time I walked through the funeral home after hours—hearing only my own footsteps and the quiet hum of the building—I felt something steady.

This mattered.

College wasn't about finding myself. It was about proving—to myself—that I could carry more than anyone expected. That I could juggle responsibility and recklessness, seriousness and humor, life and death, without dropping everything on the floor.

I didn't have it all figured out.

But I was standing upright.

And for a kid who'd once been given a one-percent chance, that felt like progress.

What I didn't know yet was how tight the timeline was about to become—or how quickly "balancing" would turn into calculation. Graduation. Marriage. Boston. All of it suddenly depended on one thing:

Getting registered early… and not falling behind.

Which is how I found myself heading to see Buddy in the registrar's office—with cash in my pocket and a plan that needed to work.

Chapter 10: Cash, Caskets, and a Company Called Marcellus

By my senior year at Texas Wesleyan, the math stopped being optional.

If I wanted to graduate on time, get married the following summer, and head to mortuary school in Boston that fall, there was only one way to do it:

Eighteen hours in the fall.

Eighteen hours in the spring.

No wiggle room. No grace period. No "we'll see how it goes."

Just a full academic load stacked on top of two jobs, a fraternity, a funeral home night schedule, a sheepdog with opinions, and a life that was already moving faster than it had any right to.

I did what any reasonable person would do.

I went to see Buddy Carter.

Buddy Carter was the longtime registrar at Texas Wesleyan, and he had been there long enough to know two things without looking at a transcript: who was serious, and who was wasting his time.

I called him first and explained my situation—that I needed to register early because I had to leave town with my father on a casket-buying trip.

There was a pause on the line. Not skeptical. Not annoyed. Just thoughtful.

Finally, he said, "Sure, Thompson. But I want cash. No checks."

He was joking. Mostly.

A few days later, I called back to see when I could come in.

"Don't forget," he said, "I want cash, Thompson."

That's when I decided to commit.

I called the business office and asked exactly how much eighteen hours plus fees would cost for the fall semester. They checked their numbers and told me:

$987.

So, I went to the bank.

And withdrew $987 in one-dollar bills.

I unbound them. Put them in a sack. Gave it a good shake, just to make sure they were well mixed.

When I walked into Buddy's office to register, we handled the paperwork, selected the classes, and he finally looked up from his desk and said, "I hope you brought cash."

I reached down beside me, lifted the sack, and poured nine hundred and eighty-seven one-dollar bills across his desk.

Buddy laughed.

I laughed.

The ladies in the office did not.

But the bill was paid.

The classes were secured.

And I was officially registered.

Sometimes, rules bend best when everyone involved understands the joke.

And that's how I found myself heading north with my father, a company called Marcellus.

If you've never been to Syracuse, NY, let me tell you what it is not.

It is not big.

It is not flashy.

And it is not impressed by you.

The Marcellus factory sits quietly in Syracuse, New York—brick buildings, solid and unassuming. The kind of place where industry once mattered deeply and still does, without needing to announce itself.

This was where caskets were built.

Not assembled.

Not outsourced.

Built.

The trip felt ceremonial. My father was in his element—focused, calm, respectful. This wasn't shopping. It was stewardship. Choosing what families would one day trust us with during their worst hours.

Inside the factory, everything slowed down.

Men worked with their hands, as craftsmen always have. Measurements mattered. Grain mattered. Hinges weren't just hinges. Linings weren't just fabric. Every detail carried weight because one day, someone would notice—and someone else would never forget.

Walking through rows of finished caskets, I was struck by how strange it was that something so beautifully constructed existed for such a solemn purpose.

There was no humor at that moment.

Just clarity.

This wasn't morbid.

It was human.

Marcellus wasn't about inventory or price lists. It was about respect—for the dead, for the living, and for the responsibility we would carry back home.

After the factory tour, we changed gears entirely.

Next stop: the Syracuse Club.

Strictly coat and tie.

Don't speak unless spoken to.

Posh beyond posh.

Lunch was with John Marcellus, Jr., the company president, who lived in the club's penthouse. To call it swanky would be a country mistake. We were accompanied by John Marcellus III, who ran the company day to day. If John Jr. represented old-world elegance and tradition, John III represented quiet authority and stewardship.

I mostly listened.

Which, in that room, was the smartest thing I could do.

After lunch, the tone shifted again. We left the city and drove about an hour out to the Marcellus Lake home on Lake Skaneateles.

That's when I realized this family didn't do anything halfway.

The house was built entirely of solid hardwoods, inside and out. Each room had its own identity—a mahogany room, a walnut room, a birch room, a cherry room, a maple room. It felt less like a house and more like a private museum of craftsmanship and restraint.

Dinner included salmon that had supposedly been caught in Alaska that morning and flown freshly.

I didn't ask questions.

Late in the afternoon, Mr. Marcellus turned to me and asked, "Do you like to water ski?"

Absolutely. I'm from Texas. Water skiing is practically a birthright.

We walked down to the boat—an old, perfectly maintained all-wood Chris-Craft—and motored out to the middle of the lake.

"Jump in," he said. "I'll throw you your skis."

I jumped.

And instantly discovered that Lake Skaneateles is not a Texas lake.

It was the coldest water I had ever been in. Not refreshing. Not bracing. Punitive.

Once I got up, I decided: I was not going to fall.

The cut signal came. I ignored it.

It came again. Still no.

There was no way I was letting go of that rope and going back into that icy hell. Eventually, physics—and gasoline—intervened, and I had no choice.

The next morning, Mr. Marcellus woke me early.

"Would you like to take a morning plunge?" he asked. "It wakes the body up."

I would rather have had one of my mother's enemas.

That day, we continued on to their private island on Lake Ontario, accessible only by boat. Even more spectacular. Even more unreal.

It was living at a level I hadn't known existed—all made possible because I worked in funeral service.

From the dead, you might say.

When we finally headed back to Texas, I wasn't just returning to school.

I was returning with resolve.

Eighteen hours waited.

So did work.

So did responsibility.

And the schedule didn't scare me anymore.

Chapter 11: The Semester My Brain Clocked In

The fall semester of my senior year at Texas Wesleyan was the first time school stopped feeling like a trick.

For most of my life, learning had felt like cracking a code I didn't have the key to. I could read the words, but they didn't always stay put. Tests felt like puzzles written in a foreign language. Half the time, I was guessing—not because I didn't care, but because I couldn't quite get there fast enough.

Then, sometime during that fall, something shifted.

Quietly. Completely. Almost without warning.

For the first time in my life, I could read a book—or a paper—and understand it. Don't memorize it. Don't fake it. Understand it. I could study and walk into a test knowing the answers. Halfway through reading a question, I already knew where it was going.

No guessing.

No decoding.

No hoping.

I just... knew.

It was exhilarating. And a little infuriating.

Because it made me wonder where that brain had been hiding all those years.

Wesleyan helped. One of the beautiful things about a small college is that professors aren't just names on a syllabus—they're people. Sometimes they were serious. Sometimes they were eccentric. Sometimes they'd walk into class, look around, and say, "Let's get out of here," and the next thing you knew, class was happening across the street at Mama's Pizza.

We'd eat pizza. We'd drink beer. We'd talk about business, economics, and life. And somehow, that counted as education.

Many of those professors became lifelong friends. Some would later become clients. Death has a way of closing loops you didn't even know were open.

Academically, I was thriving.

Personally, life was... full.

Earlier that year, my fiancée gave me an Old English Sheepdog puppy. I named him Henry.

By the fall semester, Henry was no longer a puppy. He was a presence.

Henry went to work with me at night, which meant mornings were... complicated. After getting off work, I'd race to my parents' house to get Henry settled for the day in his own little kingdom in their backyard.

I had built him an elaborate Sears shed—air conditioning, furniture, a radio, and a doggy door. It was nicer than some college apartments. My parents were not exactly dog people on my level, but they tolerated my devotion.

Barely.

Getting Henry settled and myself cleaned up usually meant I was cutting it close for my 8:00 a.m. class. I developed a system.

Every morning, I parked in a clearly marked No Parking zone for that first class. After class, I moved the car.

This resulted in a parking ticket.

Every.

Single.

Morning.

At the time, I told myself I'd deal with it later. I was very good at that.

This was also the semester I bought one of my dad's limousines—a 1976 Cadillac limo with jump seats. I removed the jump seats and had a cabinet built in their place with a TV, tape player, and a small bar setup. Because I liked making money—and because apparently sleep was optional, I rented it out.

Once or twice a week, I'd take it to Billy Bob's, park out front, and give rides for five dollars a person. We'd go down Main, around the courthouse, and back—about twenty minutes.

Henry rode shotgun.

You could say he was my service dog before service dogs were a thing.

He got more attention than I did. Including at night when we worked at the funeral home. Before going in, we'd take walks around the hospital district. At the time, the hospitals were recruiting Irish nurses who lived in the apartments behind the funeral home.

They loved Henry.

They were exceedingly cute.

They fawned all over him. I was engaged, but the flirting was harmless—and entirely canine-driven, I assure you.

Academically, everything was lining up perfectly.

I was taking five business classes and one last elective that fall—and for the first time in my life, I made straight A's.

All five.

Except for the elective class.

History Since 1960.

It was taught by a son of a Methodist bishop. A leftover hippie. Discussion only. No homework. No tests. No attendance pressure. Pass or fail.

His core belief was simple: the world was what it was because of hippies.

I believed discussion meant discussion.

I argued—politely—that in 1979, the world was rapidly becoming what it was because of computers. Even though we were just at the beginning, I could see where things were headed.

Apparently, that was not the correct answer.

At the end of the semester, my report card came.

Five A's.

And one fail.

I was stunned.

I took the grade to a professor I deeply respected, Dr. Cliff Donnelly. He walked me straight to the office of Dr. Jon Fleming, the president of Texas Wesleyan.

Dr. Fleming was equally dismayed.

He called a meeting.

In the room were Dr. Fleming, Dr. Donnelly, the hippie professor, and me.

Dr. Fleming said calmly, "I can't make you change the grade. But I don't believe it's appropriate. Would you reconsider?"

The professor said, "You're right. You can't make me change it. And I won't."

Then he stood up and walked out.

We sat there in silence.

The next day, Dr. Fleming and Dr. Donnelly called me back in.

They showed me my transcript.

The five A's were still there.

The fail was gone.

I still needed the hours.

So, in the spring, I took twenty-one hours.

Dr. Donnelly taught the class himself. There was no charge for the extra class. The requirement was simple: subscribe to The Wall Street Journal and bring an article I found interesting to his office once a week.

Sometimes we talked about it.

Sometimes he said, "Great. See you next week."

And that was that.

I didn't know it then, but looking back now, I understand something important.

Whatever my diagnosis would've been—ADD, ADHD, dyslexia—those weren't things people talked about back then. You weren't diagnosed. You were labeled.

Lazy.

Unfocused.

Not trying hard enough.

Somehow, on my own, my long-term memory finally caught up.

And once it did, there was no stopping it.

By the end of that fall, I wasn't just surviving at college.

I owned it.

Spring would bring twenty-one hours, parking tickets, graduation robes, and lessons no syllabus could prepare me for.

But that fall?

That fall was when I finally realized—

There was nothing wrong with me.

I was just early.

Chapter 12: Lordy, That Boy Graduated

By the time the spring semester arrived, there was nothing subtle left about my schedule.

I was carrying twenty-one hours, working two jobs, still pulling night duty at the funeral home, and trying to keep a large Old English Sheepdog from becoming a permanent resident of my parents' living room. If there was a way to make life easier, I apparently wasn't interested in finding it.

Somewhere in the middle of all that, graduation quietly moved from theory to problem.

The first problem was parking tickets.

Every morning, I parked in the same no-parking space for my 8:00 a.m. class. Every morning, I told myself I'd move the car right after. Every morning, the ticket was waiting for me when class ended.

I wasn't being defiant. I was tired.

Henry came to work with me at night, which meant I had to leave the funeral home early enough in the morning to get him settled at my parents' house before class. He had his own setup back there—an elaborate Sears shed I'd converted into a canine condo with air conditioning, furniture, a radio, and a doggy door. My parents were tolerant, not enthusiastic, but Henry had a way of wearing people down.

The routine left me a little late. Not dramatically late. Just late enough.

That's how you earn ninety-six parking tickets.

A couple of weeks before graduation, I was called into the Dean of Students' office. Dr. Bawcom and I were on a first-name basis. He was a good man—firm, fair, and not easily rattled.

He leaned back in his chair and said, "Martin, let me tell you a story."

He described a car that was parked every morning in a no-parking zone. Same place. At the same time. Same result.

Ticketed. Every day.

He paused. "It should've been easy to figure out who owned it," he said. "Except the car didn't have a student parking sticker."

I nodded. That part checked out.

"So, we ran the license plate," he continued. "It came back to Holiday Lincoln Mercury."

That's when I knew the gig was up.

"They informed us it was leased to a Martin Thompson."

He opened a drawer and pulled out a stack of tickets so thick it deserved its own zip code.

"Do you know how many tickets are in here?" he asked.

"About a hundred," I said.

"Ninety-six," he replied. "At ten dollars a ticket. Which means you owe us nine hundred sixty dollars before you walk across that stage."

The art of negotiation began.

We went back and forth—not adversarial, just practical. Eventually, we landed on a number that neither of us loved, but both of us could live with. We shook hands.

I paid.

I graduated.

I always liked him. I hope he liked me.

The next hurdle was the library release.

To graduate, you needed proof you didn't owe the library any books or late fees. I have been at Texas Wesleyan for four years and can say this with confidence:

I had never been to the library.

When I finally found it and walked in to request my release, the librarian looked at me the way people do when they're trying to solve a mystery that doesn't make sense.

"You've been here four years," her eyes said. "How is this possible?"

She signed the form.

Sometimes honesty really is the best policy.

Graduation day came.

As my classmates walked across the stage, the announcer rolled through distinctions—magna cum laude, summa cum laude, cum laude. My mother sat there listening carefully.

Later, she leaned over and said, "All I could think was… Lordy, that boy graduated."

Laude enough.

And that was fine.

Because by then, the next step was already underway.

I was going to mortuary school.

If I'd followed precedent, I would've gone where my brother Vic went—the Dallas Institute of Mortuary Science. It made sense. It was proven. It was familiar.

But my dad and I had other ideas.

Earlier that year, we decided to scout schools. If this was going to shape the rest of my life, we wanted to see more than one version of it. We planned a trip to Pittsburgh and Boston—two excellent schools—and, just as importantly, to funeral homes owned by some of my dad's closest friends.

First stop: Pittsburgh.

If I went there, I'd work during the week for Striffler Funeral Homes—five locations across the city. I asked why they needed so many when some seemed so close together.

"People here won't cross the river," he explained. "Race, religion, neighborhoods—it all matters."

The funeral homes were fascinating. Old, proud, deeply tied to their communities.

On weekends, I'd drive to East Liverpool, Ohio, to work for Frank Dawson. The Dawsons lived just outside town on their own tree farm, in a beautifully restored barn with a working dairy next door. You could buy fresh milk with cream still on top.

I made the mistake of shaking the bottle.

I drank what was essentially half-and-half.

Lactose intolerance made an unscheduled appearance that night.

I loved Pittsburgh. I loved East Liverpool. I loved the men who ran those places.

But we kept going.

Boston was next.

We toured the school, then visited four funeral homes where I could rotate every three months.

O'Brien's was pure Irish Catholic Boston—grand staircase, narrow building wedged between others, everything you'd expect. The staircase led to an apartment I'd live in during my time there.

The next stop was an Italian funeral home—Lamano, Panno, Fallow, or something close enough that I can still taste the dinner but can't spell the name. The funeral home was magnificent. The family dinner afterward was even better. Boston Italians know how to feed people.

Then came Waterman's—upper-class, carriage-trade Boston at its finest.

And finally, Slossberg.

An Orthodox Jewish funeral home serving over two thousand families a year in a building half the size of ours.

At first, I couldn't understand how they did it.

Then I watched.

Every ritual was exact. The preparation room was entirely wood—no metal. Rainwater collected on the roof and flowed through wooden troughs into the room for the taharah, the ritual washing performed by the Chevra Kadisha. The body was dressed in Tachrichim—simple white shrouds, equal for rich and poor alike.

Wooden tables moved through the space on a pulley system, station to station. Everything was done within twenty-four hours. Simple wooden caskets. No excess. No shortcuts.

It was fascinating in a way that rewired how I thought about funeral service.

I loved it.

Boston was it.

The plan was clear:

Graduate.

Get married that summer.

Move to Boston.

Start mortuary school in the fall.

For the first time in my life, everything lined up.

And I had no idea how fragile that certainty was.

Chapter 13: Two Cities, Two Schools, One Big Decision

That summer was supposed to be simple.

Not easy—but clear.

I was finally working full-time at the funeral home. I'd scaled back my hours at L. O. Hammons, though not entirely, mostly because I still had a rather impressive clothing bill hanging over my head. The limousine business had picked up enough to feel legitimate—actual bookings, not just late-night inspiration. I was engaged. I had a plan. And in a few short months, I'd be heading to Boston to start mortuary school.

Everything had a direction.

My fiancée had always wanted to go to Poland. She was of Polish descent and had distant family there—stories passed down, names spoken with affection but little detail. The trip was planned for three weeks. This was before international cell phones and long before casual overseas calls. The long-distance to Poland wasn't just expensive—it was an event.

So, we wrote letters.

And then, a few days before she was scheduled to return, the phone rang.

I still remember exactly where I was standing.

Her voice was calm. Not rushed. Not panicked.

"I love you," she said. "And I always will. But we can't get married."

She paused, just long enough for the words to land.

"I've met someone here. I'm staying in Poland."

There wasn't an argument. There wasn't yelling. There wasn't even confusion. Just a sudden, unmistakable understanding that everything I thought was set… wasn't.

I thanked her for calling.

And when I hung up the phone, I knew it was time to start over.

Boston no longer felt right.

Not because of fear—but because of Henry.

Boston apartments weren't built for Old English Sheepdogs. He would've been alone too much, cramped, unhappy. And if there was one thing that had been constant through every shift, every night, every hard decision, it was him.

Boston was scrapped.

It was too late to enroll at the Dallas Institute for the fall semester anyway. My brother Vic told me the spring class wasn't ideal, and I trusted his judgment. So, the plan adjusted—again.

I would work.

A lot.

I took on full-day shifts and continued nightman duty at the funeral home. I kept a few shifts at Hammons to slowly work off my clothing debt—an ironic situation, considering how well dressed I was while doing it.

That fall, Urban Cowboy hit theaters.

John Travolta changed Fort Worth overnight.

Suddenly, western wear wasn't just western, it was fashion. Hammons rolled out a high-end line that went all in hats, tailored western jackets, and boots with eel skin running all the way up the stovepipe.

I didn't ease into it.

I committed.

Hat. Clothes. Boots.

If I were single, I would be well-dressed.

Fort Worth had a place called Cowtown Country, and it became part of my routine. One night, dressed in my best Travolta interpretation, I ran into a girl I'd gone to high school with. We weren't close back then—more acquainted than anything.

She was wearing a white jumpsuit straight out of the disco era.

Without thinking too hard, I looked at her and said something along the lines of, "Is that some kind of disco outfit?"

Apparently, it worked.

We started dating. Then, I started seriously dating. Then engaged.

Life, it turns out, wasn't finished rearranging things.

We were married the following year—just before the fall class began at the Dallas Institute of Funeral Service, or DIFS, as we called it.

It wasn't the plan I'd drawn up.

But it was a plan.

And by then, I had learned something important:

When life erases the map, you don't stop moving.

You redraw it.

And you keep going.

Chapter 14: The Mortuary Student Nobody Expected

When 1981 rolled in, life decided it was time to get serious.

I got married in the fall.

I was starting mortuary school—DIFS—the day after my honeymoon.

And both marriage and school were about to put a dent in my work schedule, my sleep, and my general belief that I could do everything at once.

We got married, and then we went to Cancun.

In 1981, Cancun was still the new kid on the travel block. There were only a handful of hotels, and the Camino Real was the crown jewel—stunning, and unfortunately a bit out of my budget thanks to previous financial decisions involving cars, clothes, and an optimism that was not supported by math.

So, we stayed at the brand-new Marriott—halfway up the island and still being spruced up for an upcoming presidential visit.

Including, and I'm not making this up, hand-sanding the beach.

There weren't many restaurants yet. But there was a jet ski rental on the bay side, a bus service that ran on something like hope, and what I can only describe as an unofficial mosquito conservatory.

Early in our trip, we met an older couple—though considering I was twenty-three, "older" probably meant mid-forties. The wife was a travel agent scouting Cancun, and the husband mostly sat alone at the pool, looking like he'd been dropped into the trip as a carry-on.

One afternoon, my wife and I took a long walk down the beach. Between the Marriott and Playa Blanca was a stretch of virgin sand—almost deserted—until we stumbled onto a large group of people who had, apparently, lost their bathing suits.

Yep. A full-blown nudist beach.

We nervously laughed, turned around, and hustled back toward civilization.

And that's when I saw the lonely guy from the pool... walking straight toward the nudists like a man on a mission.

I stopped him and said, "You're not going to believe this, but there are a bunch of skinny-dippers up ahead."

He lit up and said, "Really?"

And merrily continued on his way.

I guess he was about to lose his bathing suit, too.

We got home from our honeymoon on a Sunday night in early September.

And reality hit me like a brick wall.

The next morning at 7:00 a.m., I started mortuary school.

Not only that, but I'd had to say goodbye to my job at L.O. Hammons; my full-time nightman job was now weekends only, and Dad had given me a raise so I could afford DIFS.

Oh, and did I mention I was now an instant dad to a five-year-old?

To make things even more interesting, I introduced Henry to his new home.

Henry and I had a game.

He'd take off at full speed, circle about twenty yards out, and barrel toward me like a heat-seeking missile. I'd catch his front legs, swing him to the side, and land gracefully. We'd do it again and again until he got tired.

What I forgot to do... was mention this game to my wife.

When she took Henry outside for the first time, he did what he always did: ran full speed, launched himself, and flattened her.

Then circled back and did it again.

After a few days of these impromptu NFL drills, I had to find Henry a new home.

A friend adopted him, and I could visit whenever I wanted.

I didn't know the saying "I sure miss my dog" yet… but man, I do now.

Chapter 15: Learning Death the Right Way

If college taught me how to balance, mortuary school taught me how to endure.

The Dallas Institute of Funeral Service—DIFS, as everyone called it—didn't care who your father was, how many funerals you'd worked, or how confident you felt walking in the door. The building itself looked like it had been tired since the Eisenhower administration, and I'm certain nothing inside had been updated since then, either.

Classes ran Monday through Friday, 7:30 a.m. to 12:30 p.m. Sharp. Miss enough mornings, and nobody chases you down; you simply disappeared. DIFS didn't babysit. It filtered.

The student center was a museum of neglect. Torn vinyl chairs that had seen better decades. A pool table missing enough felt to turn every shot into a theological debate. A ping-pong table with a crack straight down the middle, guaranteeing that no game ever ended peacefully.

There was no cafeteria. No breakroom. No illusion that nutrition mattered.

Instead, twice a day, salvation arrived on wheels.

We called it the Roach Coach.

It parked outside like an armored vehicle and offered a menu that required faith. I once ordered a chicken sandwich. What arrived was neither chicken nor particularly sandwich-like. From that day forward, I stuck to items that couldn't be misrepresented—Cokes, chips, and things wrapped so tightly in foil they couldn't escape responsibility.

After class, I didn't head home.

I headed back to Fort Worth.

That's where the rest of my life was still happening.

I worked afternoons and evenings at Thompson's Harveson & Cole, and every third night I was on call. That meant that somewhere around

2:00 a.m., the phone would ring, and the new nightman would be on the other end, saying something along the lines of, "We've got a removal."

I'd get dressed, make the call, bring the person into our care, embalm, clean up, and head home just in time to shower and drive forty-plus miles back to Dallas for class.

It was a schedule designed by someone who hated sleep.

I ran on caffeine, adrenaline, and the quiet knowledge that quitting wasn't an option. I wasn't just learning embalming techniques; I was learning how to function when tired, how to focus when exhausted, and how to keep my hands steady even when my body wanted to stop.

This was funeral service, old-school style.

And somehow, in the middle of all that, I was still running my limousine business.

One night, I got booked to drive a doctor and his much younger girlfriend from Fort Worth to Dallas. The itinerary was ambitious: Neiman Marcus first, then dinner at The French Room in the Adolphus, then back home.

While they were shopping, the doctor asked me to buy a Polaroid camera and extra film.

I didn't ask why. At that point in my life, asking fewer questions felt like a survival skill.

I bought the camera, returned to Neiman's, and waited in my navy-blue Cadillac limousine. When they finished dinner, I pulled out from the curb—only to discover Dallas had just installed brand-new NO TURN signs.

I reasoned, incorrectly, that "No Turn" surely didn't apply to a one-way street turning onto another one-way street.

It did.

Red and blue lights filled my mirror.

"Do you know why I pulled you over?" the officer asked.

I said, "Because I made a legal turn?"

He said, "Nope. New law. No turns. Period."

I got two tickets.

As I stood there, absorbing this information, the doctor stepped out of the limo, holding the Polaroid camera, and started taking pictures.

Of me.

Of the officer.

Of the officer writing the ticket.

I was too tired to react.

Dallas had something called Night Court, which meant if you got a ticket at night, you could fight it before sunrise. My hearing was scheduled for 3:00 a.m.

After finishing the limo run, I drove straight to Night Court. The judge listened, sighed, and reduced it to one ticket.

I paid more in fines than I made that night.

A week later, the doctor handed me an envelope.

Inside were Polaroids.

I'm standing next to the cop.

A close-up of the ticket.

The cop mid-sentence.

His girlfriend was laughing in the back seat.

"If you ever want to remember your first Night Court experience," he said, "these should help."

Mortuary school didn't teach that lesson—but life did.

By the end of that first stretch at DIFS, I understood something clearly:

This wasn't about textbooks, buildings, or even grades.

It was about stamina.

It was about responsibility.

It was about learning how to show up when you were tired, unsure, and stretched thin—and doing the job anyway.

Somewhere between the Roach Coach, a 2:00 a.m. removal, and a Polaroid camera in a Dallas streetlight, I stopped feeling like someone learning funeral service.

I started feeling like someone living it.

Interlude: A Very Quick History of Funeral Service

(For people who didn't wake up this morning hoping to hear about mummies, rum, and the FTC)

Before we go any further, I probably owe you a little context.

Because if you've never worked in a funeral home, the whole thing can feel like a foreign country—same language, totally different customs. And if you have worked in one, you already know: funeral service is one of the only professions where people can watch you do everything right… and still say, "Well, I hope I never need you."

Fair.

Now, I've actually written an entire book about the history of funeral service—Heart and Humanity—from the beginning of time up through the modern era. If you're the kind of person who enjoys the "how we got here" part of life, you'd probably like it. But for this book, I'm not going to drop a full history textbook in the middle of the story.

We're going to do the short version.

And by "short," I mean I'm going to tell it the way I used to tell it when my dad shoved me into public speaking long before I was ready.

How I Learned Funeral Service Might Be the Oldest Profession

When I was in my early twenties and working full-time under my dad's watchful eye, he informed me one day that I was going to give a speech to the Serra Club—a room full of respected Catholic men, many of whom were Fort Worth's movers and shakers.

You want to know what's terrifying?

Speaking to a group of successful men when you're young, undertrained, and still trying to figure out whether your tie is straight. Speaking to them about death is a whole other level of panic.

So, I did what anyone in funeral service does when they're nervous: I over-prepared for the worst.

I wrote my speech. I rehearsed it. I practiced in the mirror. And then I decided, at the last second, I'd start with humor—because if you can get a room to laugh, you can buy yourself about three minutes of grace.

I opened with something like:

"Gentlemen, thank you for having me. I'd like to begin with a brief history of funeral service. We like to think of ourselves as the oldest profession… even though I know another profession claims that title. I just like to believe we're held in slightly higher regard."

That line usually got a laugh.

Then I went through a phase where I tried to get fancy and use the Bible as a prop—Genesis, Cain and Abel, the whole deal. I'd flip it open and say:

"The first recorded funeral service is right here. Cain and Abel. After Cain took care of Abel, Adam and Eve called Guy Thompson to handle the arrangements."

Now… sometimes that landed.

And sometimes it landed like a lead balloon, dying right there in the room.

After enough of those, I retired the Bible bit for my own emotional health. I decided the Lord had heard enough from me and preferred I keep it simple.

Here's the simple version—the version that matters for this story:

People Have Always Needed Someone

Death has been around since the beginning of time. And even before we had funeral homes, somebody had to decide:

What do we do with the body?

How do we honor the person?

How do we help the living survive what just happened?

That's the heart of funeral service. It always has been.

The methods change. The terminology changes. The rules change.

But the basic human need to care for someone in the end and for the family left behind hasn't changed one bit.

The "Original Embalmers" Weren't who I thought.

For years, I'd start my history talk with Ancient Egypt—because, honestly, mummies make good material.

The Egyptians practiced embalming like an art form. Organs removed and preserved. Bodies dried, treated, wrapped, and prepared for the afterlife. They believed the body mattered. They believed the soul mattered. They believed what happened next mattered.

Then I learned something that made me adjust my little speech.

Turns out, the Egyptians weren't first.

Long before the pyramids, people in South America, associated with the Chinchorro culture, practiced mummification thousands of years earlier. And what's wild is they didn't reserve it for royalty or the wealthy. They did it for everyone—men, women, children, even infants.

Equal opportunity embalming.

Which is a phrase I never thought I'd say, but here we are.

If you want the truth: funeral service has always been both practical and deeply human. Even early civilizations understood: if someone mattered in life, they should still be treated with care in death.

The Romans Turned Funerals into Theater

Then you get the Romans.

The Romans didn't do subtle.

They held processions, torchlight ceremonies, and funerals that reflected the person's status. If you were important, your funeral was important. If you were very important, it was a full production.

And yes, in many places and periods, cremation was common. That surprises some people, because today we act like cremation is a "new thing."

It isn't.

What's new isn't cremation, it's how modern America argues about it.

Colonial America: "Come for the Wake, Stay for the Rum"

Now this part always makes people laugh, because it doesn't match the image we have of early America.

We picture buckle hats and seriousness.

But early American funerals—especially the wakes—were often social events. People gathered in homes. They kept watch. They ate. They drank.

In some cases, the liquor bill could compete with the funeral costs.

It got so excessive in some places that laws were passed to stop the "extravagance" of funeral spending—especially the gift-giving and the alcohol.

So yes: there was a time in America when legislators looked at funerals and thought, we've got to regulate the rum.

If the FTC had existed then, they would've started with whiskey.

The Civil War Changed Everything

Here's where funeral service begins to look more like what we recognize.

Before embalming became common, most families buried quickly because decomposition doesn't wait for your feelings. And transporting someone over a distance? That was difficult.

Then came the Civil War.

Thousands of young men died far from home, and families wanted them brought back. That demand pushed embalming forward in a very practical way.

And when President Lincoln was assassinated and his body traveled by train with public viewings along the way, embalming became something the public saw up close. It helped normalize the idea that preservation and viewing could be part of the mourning process.

Modern embalming didn't spring out of nowhere. It developed because families needed time to gather, to say goodbye, and to make sense of their loss.

From "Undertaker" to "Funeral Director"

For a long time, funerals were held at home. Family and community did what needed to be done. Eventually, tradesmen—furniture makers, carpenters—began making coffins, then providing additional services, and eventually coordinating the whole thing.

That's where the term undertaker came from: someone who "undertook" the responsibility.

Later, we became morticians (which sounds like a magician with a darker wardrobe), and later still, funeral directors, because the job became less about physical logistics and more about directing a process: helping families navigate choices, grief, faith, and practicality all at once.

And yes—our profession can't stop renaming itself.

Undertaker. Mortician. Funeral director. Funeral arranger. End-of-life specialist.

At this rate, one day they'll call us "Celebration Logistics Officers" and hand us a lanyard.

Then Jessica Mitford Walked in and Lit the Match

In the 1960s, the funeral profession took a public hit—big time—when Jessica Mitford published The American Way of Death and painted funeral directors as polished salesmen preying on grief.

Now, I'm not going to pretend there weren't bad actors in the profession. Every industry has them.

But most funeral directors I've known, especially the ones who stayed in the business for decades, were not villains. They were hardworking, sleep-deprived, stubborn, service-minded people who believed deeply in doing things right.

Still, Mitford's book had an effect. It changed how the public viewed funeral costs, and it helped lead to the FTC Funeral Rule, which required transparency: itemized pricing, consumer rights, and fewer opportunities for confusion.

Bottom line? Families deserved clarity.

And funeral directors had to adjust.

The Biggest Shift of all: Cremation

When I started, "traditional funeral" was basically the default setting. Two-day visitation. Church service. Burial.

Cremation existed, but it was rare.

Then, over time, cremation became more common—for lots of reasons: cost, mobility, changing religious views, and the fact that families weren't living in the same town for six generations anymore.

And funeral homes had to learn something important:

Choosing cremation doesn't mean a family doesn't want a ceremony.

It doesn't mean they don't want meaning.

It doesn't mean they don't want to gather.

It just means the "how" changed.

Where we are now

Today, you've got livestreaming, online memorials, green burials, aquamation, personalization, and families doing things their own way.

Some of it is beautiful.

Some of it is… creative.

And some of it makes old-school funeral directors squint like they're trying to read tiny print without their glasses.

But here's what hasn't changed:

People still need help when someone dies.

They still need dignity.

They still need care.

They still need someone steady in the room.

And that's why funeral service has survived everything from mummies to modern technology.

Because it's not really about the method.

It's about the moment.

The man who taught me

Where It All Started for Me: Harveson & Cole and the Man Who Taught Me Everything

Now that I've taken you from mummies to Mitford in about the time it takes most people to microwave leftover spaghetti, let me zoom back in.

Because funeral history is interesting—but what really matters in this book is how I ended up in the middle of it, in Fort Worth, working for the one man who could intimidate you with a look… and make a grieving family feel safe with the very same look.

That story starts with Harveson & Cole.

Harveson & Cole was founded in 1911 by a retired railroad man named Quincy Adams Harveson. And before you ask—yes, that's a presidential name. You'll notice a theme around here. Fort Worth was full of hardworking folks, but the funeral home business apparently required a little extra patriotism.

Quincy worked around the main train station and befriended a man who owned Sloane Mortuary. Then Fort Worth got hit with a deadly disease, and that owner suffered the kind of loss that can break a person: he buried his wife… and then, one by one, nearly his entire family.

Quincy helped him do it.

And after the last funeral, the owner handed Quincy the keys and said, in so many words, "I'm done."

That's a detail that still gets me, because it's the kind of moment you can't fake. Grief can be heavy enough to end a life even if you're still living it.

So, Quincy took over. The business became Sloane and Harveson, and over time, it evolved into Harveson & Cole when Quincy's daughter married Grover Cleveland Cole.

Yes—another presidential name. If we had one more, we could've started our own Mount Rushmore.

Back then, funeral services didn't happen in a "funeral home" the way we picture it today. Most funerals were held at the family home. The funeral home was more like an office and a supply base. You went out to the home, did what you needed to do, and helped the family through it right there in their living room.

By the 1920s, families started shifting away from home funerals. People wanted a dedicated place for wakes and services, so Harveson & Cole expanded into the Masonic Lodge on Magnolia, renting the basement first, then the first and second floors.

And here's something I love because it shows how practical funeral directors had to be: like many mortuaries in those days, they ran side businesses to survive. Harveson & Cole operated a private switchboard—an early version of an answering service.

And before pagers, before cell phones, before anyone could text "u up?"—they even used a flag system downtown. If a doctor was urgently needed, someone would hang a specific flag out of a window and hope he saw it and called in.

It wasn't perfect, but it was genius for the time.

We were basically emergency communication… with laundry.

That's the kind of funeral home Harveson & Cole was: part funeral service, part civic support system, part "whatever the community needs next."

Then, after World War II, the story takes a turn that matters to me.

Because that's when my dad showed up.

Guy Thompson: The Man Who Taught Me Everything

My dad, Guy Thompson, didn't grow up in funeral service. He grew up working—period.

He was the son of a milkman and a chicken farmer on the Northside of Fort Worth. Money was tight. Work was constant. And somehow, with all that, Dad graduates valedictorian and earns a full ride to the University of Texas.

Everybody thought he'd be a doctor or a lawyer or something sensible.

Instead, he got fascinated by funeral service after a death in the family—and the day after graduation, he walked into a funeral home and asked for a job.

The funeral director told him, "Guy, I'd be doing you a disservice keeping you from your future."

Most people would've taken the hint.

Dad went home, decided he'd shown up wrong, and the next day he went downtown to Washer Brothers and bought himself a suit—shirt, tie, shoes, all of it—for five dollars.

Five dollars.

That suit may have been the best investment our family ever made.

He walked into the fanciest funeral home in town—Robertson Mueller Harper—and asked again. They said they didn't have openings.

Dad said, "Mind if I clean up your sidewalks and weed your flowerbeds until you do?"

That was Dad in one sentence: no ego, all hustle.

Two weeks later, they hired him.

He went to mortuary school in Dallas and commuted in a way that sounds like a punishment now—bus, train, bus, class, reverse it, work the rest of the day. He graduated at the top of his class, then hit a tiny snag:

He was too young to be licensed.

You had to be eighteen.

He was seventeen and a half.

He petitioned the commission and somehow—through persistence, charm, and probably that $5 suit again—he got licensed anyway.

Then World War II came along, and Dad joined the Navy. He studied, advanced, and even when he was on leave—this part always makes me shake my head—he'd walk into funeral homes in whatever city he was in and volunteer to help.

Who does that?

Guy Thompson.

After the war, he ends up at Harveson & Cole, becomes manager, and brings with him a large part of the Catholic business in Fort Worth. Now, serving Catholic families out of a Masonic Lodge wasn't exactly seamless, so Dad knew the firm had to move if it was going to grow.

So, in 1957, Dad purchased the big house on 8th Avenue, along with neighboring properties, and converted it into what became Fort Worth's finest funeral home for decades.

Harveson & Cole stayed there until I moved us in 2020, because—just like I told you in Part A—funeral service never stops evolving.

And the name "Thompson's"? We didn't add that until 1980.

It took a while… but eventually, our family name made it onto the door.

Why am I telling you all this?

Because when you read the next chapters—when you see me working nights, learning the trade, trying to find my footing—you need to understand something:

I wasn't just learning funeral service.

I was learning it under a man who treated it like a calling, ran it like a discipline, and believed deeply that families deserved excellence—whether they were Catholic, Baptist, Jewish, rich, broke, or somewhere in between.

And I can tell you right now:

That man taught me everything.

Which brings us back to me—full-time at Harveson & Cole—staring at the big board like it was holy scripture… except this scripture came with flower vans, church schedules, and a father who could detect laziness from three rooms away.

Chapter 16: The Night Shift Teaches You Everything

Graduating from mortuary school was supposed to be my grand entrance into full-time funeral service.

It was.

It was also my gateway into a whole new world of golf, friendly gambling, and one nickname that has clung to me for decades like embalming fluid on a bad day.

When I walked out of school for the last time, I swear I heard the heavenly choir. No more tests. No more lectures. No more pretending I had read something I absolutely had not read.

Well… almost.

Before I could officially call myself a Funeral Director and Embalmer, I still had one final hurdle: Austin.

The state board exam.

This was the big one—funeral directing and embalming—everything rolled into one exam that basically asked, "Alright, kid… You sure you want to do this?"

By then, I had eighteen years of education under my belt, and for the first time in my life, I had finally learned how to study. Not "panic the night before," not "skim and pray," but actual, legitimate studying.

And I'll be honest: I did great.

I passed. I was official. And I was now working full-time in funeral service with a real paycheck and a schedule that wasn't built by Satan and the Dallas Tollway.

That's when I did something I'd wanted to do for years.

I joined a country club.

Picking a Club (Without Shady Oaks Money)

If you lived in Fort Worth and you were serious about golf, there were a few clubs that carried a little extra prestige.

Shady Oaks—Ben Hogan territory, and my brother was a member.

Colonial—where you could practically hear the golf history whispering in your backswing.

Ridglea—two great courses.

River Crest—blue-bloods, and if you weren't born into it, good luck.

And then there was Woodhaven.

Woodhaven wasn't trying to be River Crest. Woodhaven was a working man's club. Good golf. Good people. Good games. A place where you didn't have to pretend you were somebody's cousin just to get through the front door.

Even though I was making what I thought was good money, it wasn't Shady Oaks money. So, I joined Woodhaven.

Best decision I ever made.

Work and school had kept me away from golf for years, but all of a sudden, I had something I hadn't had in a long time:

A little breathing room.

And I filled it with golf.

Woodhaven had a standing game every weekday except Monday, plus Saturday mornings and Sunday afternoons.

They called it "the gangsome."

And if you've never been around a gangsome, let me describe it: it's equal parts golf game, social club, therapy session, and mild gambling operation.

It was rowdy. Competitive. Welcoming. And the kind of group that could give you a hard time and make you feel like family in the very same sentence.

Most of those guys were in their forties, fifties, and sixties. The youngest guy—other than me—was probably mid-thirties. I was about twenty-four, and it looked like I needed permission to order a beer.

It didn't matter.

They welcomed me anyway.

And before long, I was playing golf like I'd made up for lost time... because I was.

This is where I met Eddie Robinson.

If you grew up around baseball, you knew who Eddie was. Major League player in the 1940s and '50s, later became the General Manager of the Texas Rangers, and even in retirement, he stayed involved as a scout.

Woodhaven had a few former Rangers players around, too, so some days that golf game felt like I'd wandered into a locker room where everybody had a better swing and a better story than I did.

One day, they were calling out teams, and I heard somebody yell:

"I've got Digger!"

I remember standing there thinking, Digger? Who the hell is Digger?

Then I realized... he was looking at me.

Turns out, the name came from Digger O'Dell, "the friendly undertaker" from an old radio and TV show called The Life of Riley.

They even quoted him—because of course they did:

"It is I, Digby O'Dell, the friendly undertaker."

Now I'll be honest—when you're a young guy trying to be taken seriously, you don't know how you feel about being assigned a nickname that sounds like a cartoon character.

But when you're the only funeral director in a golf group full of retired baseball players and lifelong gamblers, you don't get to hold a committee meeting about it.

I did what I always do.

I embraced it.

And just like that… "Digger" stuck.

I have been called many things in my life. Some of them were flattering. Some of them were creative. Some of them are not fit for print, in a book a decent person might buy.

But "Digger"? I could live with that.

I liked it.

Woodhaven wasn't just golf. It was a whole education.

Those guys taught me how to play gin.

They ran a casino game once a week.

They taught me the fine art of friendly betting—meaning it was "friendly" right up until you missed a three-footer for five bucks.

They also taught me something my father never covered in mortuary school:

If you're supposed to be home at 6:00 p.m. and you walk in at 8:30…

You'd better have one heck of an excuse.

Or a good bottle of wine.

Or both.

And even then, don't act surprised if your bride looks at you like she's considering a private graveside service.

Looking back, Woodhaven wasn't about status.

It was about belonging.

It was about older men who had been through life—war stories, career stories, marriage stories, divorce stories—and were willing to take a young guy under their wing and let him learn by being present.

They gave me laughter when my days could get heavy.

They gave me friendship when life was shifting fast.

They gave me a place to breathe.

And they gave me a nickname that followed me into every stage of life after that.

Digger had arrived.

And he wasn't going anywhere.

Chapter 17: Maybe Too Optimistic

That's not what you're supposed to say about a civic organization devoted to community service... but let's be honest.

When you're twenty-three, fresh out of mortuary school, newly married, trying to prove you're a real adult, you don't wake up thinking, you know what I need? Volunteer work and committee meetings.

You go where somebody invites you. You go where the older guys are. You go where the lunch is good. And if we're being completely honest, you go where there's a decent chance somebody might throw some business your way.

That's how I wound up at the Fort Worth Optimist Club.

They met every Friday at noon at First United Methodist Church downtown. And the first thing I noticed was this:

Those folks could cook.

Roast beef that didn't taste like it came out of a cafeteria warming drawer. Mashed potatoes that had been mixed with butter. Sweet tea that didn't feel like it had been poured straight out of a hummingbird feeder.

It was the kind of lunch that made you think I could get used to civic duty.

And to be fair, there was a real civic duty happening.

"Friend of Youth" Wasn't Just a Motto

The Optimist Club wasn't a bunch of men in sport coats congratulating themselves over lunch. They were genuinely committed to kids in Fort Worth. Their motto, "Friend of Youth," wasn't a slogan—they lived it.

They had on-campus programs at elementary schools. They ran junior golf tournaments to introduce kids to the game. And they sponsored a Little League baseball program for underprivileged kids on the Southside that was the real deal.

Those boys played for free. They got brand-new hats and shirts. Their team photos were covered. And at the end of every game, each kid got a treat—whatever he wanted.

I loved that. I was proud to be part of it.

But programs like that don't run on good intentions.

They run on money.

Which means fundraisers.

And the Optimists had two big ones:

The Christmas Tree Sale

One green tree lot at Lancaster and University.

One flocked tree lot inside Will Rogers Coliseum.

And if you ever saw a giant snow-covered tree in a bank lobby or a Fort Worth hotel… there's a good chance we sold it to them.

The Annual Charity Golf Tournament

Which, if we're being honest, was also a great excuse for a bunch of business guys to drink beer and claim it was "for the children."

Between my new membership and my growing friendship with Eddie Robinson, I was all in.

And that's how I made my first major mistake.

The Day I Became Program Chair (A Warning Story)

Somebody asked me to be the program chair.

When someone asks you that, you assume it's important. Like you're getting promoted. Like you've been recognized.

It's not.

Program chair just means you are responsible for lining up a guest speaker every Friday—except Easter, Christmas, and New Year's—so the club has something to do between saying the prayer and attacking the dessert.

It sounds simple until you burn through the obvious speakers.

And I burned through them fast.

After a while, I found myself staring at the phone, as if it would call me with a solution.

That's when I made a decision that should've required a sobriety test.

I invited Tarrant County's new medical examiner, Dr. Peerwani, to speak.

He seemed like a nice guy. Professional. Polished. He even requested a projector and a screen.

I should have known right then that my roast beef days were numbered.

Friday, 12:30 p.m. — The luncheon that ended the appetite

It was a normal Friday.

The lunch was fantastic. The room was full. Men were joking, visiting, shaking hands, doing all the Optimist things.

Then Dr. Peerwani stepped to the podium and announced his topic:

"The Role of the Medical Examiner in Forensic Science."

That sounded educational.

Then the slides started.

Slide one: a decomposed body in a shallow grave.

I heard silverware pause.

Slide two: a gunshot victim from point-blank range.

A couple of men shifted in their seats.

Slide three: a bloated corpse pulled from the Trinity River.

Somebody's fork clinked against a plate like it had given up.

Slide four: a suicide victim with a particularly… dramatic exit wound.

That's when the first man stood up and walked out.

Then another.

And another.

By slide six, half the room was gone.

By slide ten, the ones still sitting were in one of three categories:

genuinely interested in forensic pathology,

too stubborn to leave, or

holding down their lunch through sheer force of will.

By the end of the presentation, it was me, the speaker, and a handful of men who looked like they'd aged five years in forty minutes.

Dr. Peerwani, meanwhile, was thrilled.

He thanked us for being such a great audience and said he'd be happy to come back anytime.

The club president stood up, shook his hand, smiled politely, and said:

"That won't be necessary."

And just like that, I became the only person in Fort Worth history to turn an Optimist Club luncheon into an involuntary diet program.

And Then There Was the Belly Dancer

You would think one civic club disaster would have been enough.

You would be wrong.

Somewhere between the medical examiner incident and my phone ringing off the hook as I'd just canceled Christmas, a few of the younger guys in the club—and I use the word "younger" loosely—pulled me aside.

They told me there was an annual program everyone loved. A crowd favorite. Something "fun."

All the details had already been handled, they said.

The speaker was booked.

The fee was covered.

"All you have to do," they said, "is put it on the schedule."

I was young.

I was gullible.

And apparently, I was still learning that when men say everyone looks forward to it, you should ask who everyone is.

Friday came.

The lunch crowd was full.

Several pastors were present.

We were, once again, inside First United Methodist Church.

The program began.

Music cued.

And that's when I realized—about two seconds too late—that this was not, in fact, a cultural presentation.

What followed was a performance that started as professional belly dancing and slowly—but confidently—crossed the line into something far more appropriate for a smoky nightclub than a church fellowship hall.

There was hip movement.

There was audience interaction.

There was tipping.

Yes. Tipping.

As she danced near the tables, a few men—men who had known me since I was a kid—were being invited to tuck bills into her waistband.

And that's when I felt it.

That slow, synchronized turning of heads.

The looks.

Have you lost your mind? Looks.

This is your fault.

Guy Thompson's son has finally snapped.

I scanned the room in a mild panic—and that's when I saw them.

My so-called friends.

Standing in the back.

Laughing.

Barely holding it together.

There had never been an annual program like this.

Not ever.

This was not traditional.

This was a setup.

I had been played by a group of grown men who decided it would be fun to see how much damage a young, well-meaning program chair could do in under ten minutes.

Déjà Vu, Only Louder

My phone rang all afternoon.

Pastors.

Members.

Concerned Optimists.

People who had never called me before and probably never would again.

It sounded suspiciously familiar—almost exactly like the medical examiner aftermath, except now nobody was nauseated.

They were offended.

Eventually, my "friends" fessed up. Mostly because I was taking real heat, and they realized I might not survive another luncheon.

Then the story inevitably reached my father.

And if you think being scolded by civic leaders is uncomfortable, try explaining belly dancing at a Methodist church to Guy Thompson.

Anything bad that happened in public had a way of following me back to the office.

It was like grade school all over again, except now the punishment involved silence, disappointment, and the sense that you had somehow embarrassed multiple generations at once.

The truly amazing part?

They didn't remove me as program chair.

Apparently, the Optimist Club was either very forgiving… or very desperate.

File This Away for Later

I stayed.

I behaved.

And I learned two very important lessons:

Never trust anyone who says, "Everybody loves this program."

Revenge, when timed correctly, is far more satisfying than immediate retaliation.

Because years later—when the moment was just right—I got my revenge.

And it was spectacular.

Now, by then, thanks to Woodhaven, I was already getting used to being called "Digger."

But apparently, the world felt like I deserved options.

Over the years, I've collected nicknames like most people collect golf balls in the water:

"Buddy" — because my twin sister couldn't pronounce Martin.

"Marty" — my mom's idea (I hated it).

"Marty Farty" — a bean-heavy childhood disaster that a few cousins still think is adorable.

"Rug Beater" — given to me by a retired LPGA pro at Woodhaven because my swing offended her spiritually.

"Pink Flamingo" — thanks to one unfortunate pair of pastel pink shorts and legs so skinny I could've been issued wading permits.

But "Digger" stuck.

And after the Dr. Peerwani luncheon, I'm just grateful they didn't rename me "Appetite Killer."

Lessons from the Optimist Club (and the Worst Luncheon Ever)

Never say yes to being program chair unless you have a full Rolodex of speakers.

Forensic pathology is best discussed when people are not eating.

Nicknames are forever—choose your clothing carefully.

And if you ever invite a medical examiner to speak at lunch… at least warn people first.

Because nothing ruins roast beef faster than a slideshow that looks like a Crime Scene Unit highlight reel.

Chapter 18: 1984: It's a Boy

1984 wasn't the rollercoaster that 1980 was, but it still changed my life in two completely different ways.

First, I finished my apprenticeship — the final lap before I could be fully licensed. I had one last test to pass, and by then it felt like a formality… the kind that still makes you sweat through your shirt.

When the results came in, I'd done it.

I was officially a Licensed Funeral Director and Embalmer.

Or, if you prefer the more dramatic title — the one people still use when they want to sound like a character in a black-and-white movie — I was a Licensed Mortician.

And it happened with all the celebration and pageantry of getting your license renewed at the DMV.

No ceremony.

No speech.

No moment where angels sang, and someone handed me a gold-plated embalming machine.

Just a piece of paper… and a reminder that every two years I'd need sixteen hours of continuing education.

So apparently, "graduating" was just a concept. Not a reality.

But the truth is, the license wasn't the big story of 1984.

The big story was that Jon was born.

Since it was a scheduled C-section, I knew the time and day, which didn't make it any less surreal. I was standing in an operating room in scrubs, trying to look calm and helpful… while also trying not to be the guy who passes out and becomes a second patient.

The doctor worked for a few minutes, lifted his head, and said the words that changed everything:

"It's a boy."

Just like that, the world shifted.

My wife and I had made a deal: she'd name a girl; I'd name a boy. It sounded fair at the time — like something you can negotiate rationally before sleep deprivation and diapers show up.

At first, I leaned toward John Paul.

Then I caught myself and thought, " Do I really want people assuming I'm running some kind of personal fan club for the Pope? Not that I had anything against the Pope… I just didn't want to spend the next eighteen years answering questions about it.

I went with Jon — inspired by two men I admired: Dr. Jon Fleming, the president of Texas Wesleyan, and Jon Brumley, a good neighbor and a steady example of the kind of man I respected.

Middle name David.

Why David?

Because it sounded right.

Because it didn't come with any papal associations.

And because if Jon ever decided he didn't like his first name, he'd at least have a solid option waiting in the wings.

Of course, what I didn't realize was that I had just guaranteed my son a lifetime of:

"Jon with no 'H.' Yes… really. No 'H.'"

But none of that mattered when I saw him.

I'd loved my Old English Sheepdog, Henry, like family. He'd been my loyal companion — my co-pilot, my shadow, my constant.

But this was different.

This was a new kind of love. The kind that rearranges your priorities without asking your permission.

From that day forward, I knew it in a way I'd never known anything before:

I'd give my life for my son.

1980 may have been wild and unpredictable.

But 1984?

That was the year everything truly began.

Chapter 19: SL 500

After 1984, life settled into a pretty good rhythm: wake up, shower, get dressed, go to work.

Not exactly the plot of an action movie — but I had upgraded from a station wagon to one of our navy-blue Cadillac Broughams, so I felt like I was doing fine.

And yes, the entire fleet had moved from Briar Rose — those pink cars that tested the limits of my masculinity — to dignified navy blue.

I consider myself a secure man.

But there are limits.

My brother Vic drove a Suburban, and we even replaced the old station-wagon first-call cars with Suburban's, too. Mom finally spared the indignity of being seen in what looked like a rolling reminder of the 1970s.

Things were good.

And then Christmas rolled around, and Dad decided it was time to buy Mom a new car.

Now, my father wasn't what you'd call a "car guy," but he had a unique way of describing what he wanted.

He said, casually, "Your mother likes those cars with numbers and letters on the back."

Numbers and letters?

"Yeah," he said, "something like a 500SL."

I stopped and looked at him.

"Dad... do you even know what that is?"

"I don't care," he said. "Just go find one."

So off I went to the Mercedes dealership on the west side of Fort Worth.

And there it was: a beautiful white 500SL. Sleek. Luxurious. The kind of car that says, " We have arrived, even if you're just driving to the grocery store.

I called Dad.

"Have them wire Bank of Commerce for payment," he said.

"Dad... do you know how much these cars cost?"

"I'm sure it's somewhere around ten thousand."

"No, sir. It's thirty thousand."

Silence.

A long pause.

Then he said, calmly and firmly:

"Come straight back here."

And just like that, the dream of numbers-and-letters luxury vanished.

Instead, Mom ended up with a black Chrysler Fifth Avenue.

It wasn't exactly a status symbol, but it did have words instead of numbers and letters, which I guess made it easier to spell. Dad could live with that.

The problem was… it was a lemon.

A sour, mechanical disaster that taught us an important lesson:

Sometimes numbers and letters really do mean something.

Mom got a new car.

Dad got a story that would live forever.

And I learned a rule that has served me well ever since:

Never let Dad go car shopping based on a hunch.

Chapter 20: What Not to Say at a Funeral

If you want a perfect snapshot of early fatherhood, it's this:

I rented Ghostbusters one night, thinking it would be a fun movie.

I didn't realize I was introducing a lifestyle.

The moment the credits rolled, Jon looked at me and said, "Let's watch it again."

So, we did.

Repeatedly, to the point where I'm pretty sure the video store considered giving me a key and putting my name on a shelf.

Eventually, common sense kicked in, and I bought the movie.

Jon didn't just watch Ghostbusters.

He became one.

He had the outfit. The proton pack. The whole deal. And he wore it every single day like it was his uniform, and the neighborhood was under constant supernatural threat.

At night, while he slept in Ghostbuster pajamas, we'd sneak the real jumpsuit into the wash. By morning, it was clean and ready for duty.

I loved every second of it.

Then came sports.

When Jon turned four, signs went up all over the neighborhood: soccer sign-ups.

We walked into the rec center, and the guy behind the table told me, "All the teams are full… but we have a group of kids who want to play if we can find a coach."

And something stirred inside me.

A calling.

A destiny.

You see, as a child, I was fully convinced that I was meant to be a professional kickball player.

So, I thought: Soccer is basically kickball with shin guards. I'm your guy.

"I'll coach," I said.

There was just one small problem:

I knew absolutely nothing about soccer.

Growing up in Texas, soccer wasn't exactly a thing. Grade school — no team. High school — no team. College — no team. And for Dallas, getting a professional soccer team? That was still years away.

But I wasn't going to let reality ruin my confidence.

I did what I always did when I didn't know what I was doing:

I went to the library, and I guess this was the first time for me.

I checked out every book I could find. I studied. I memorized terms. I was ready to turn this group of four-year-olds into a World Cup machine.

Then the practice started.

And within five minutes, I realized I had wasted a whole lot of time.

There was no strategy.

No formations.

No brilliant coaching.

All they really needed was kick the ball.

And if, by some miracle, they kicked it in the right direction — bonus.

Game day was controlled chaos. Kids running in circles. Occasional collisions. The ball is rolling around like an afterthought.

And when the other team managed to advance toward our goal, I'd look over at my goalie…

...who was usually sitting in the grass, playing with weeds, completely unaware that a sporting event was happening.

We didn't win much.

But nobody cared.

The kids had a blast.

And honestly? So, did I.

Then baseball sign-ups came, and somehow, I fell for the same trick.

"We need a coach."

"Sure. I'll coach."

Basketball? Fine.

Football? Why not?

By that point, I figured if enthusiasm was the only requirement, I was headed for the Coaching Hall of Fame.

But the real reason I kept saying yes had nothing to do with soccer, baseball, or any sport.

It had everything to do with Jon.

I wanted to be there.

On the sidelines. On the field. In the moments.

Because that's what mattered.

And if coaching sports, I didn't understand, was the price of admission for more time with my son...

Sign me up.

Again, and again, and again.

Chapter 21: South Padre or Bust

While other kids were heading off to Disneyland, summer camp, or anywhere that involved sunshine and fun, our family vacations had a different destination altogether: the Texas Funeral Directors Association convention.

Because what kid doesn't dream of spending summer surrounded by caskets, hearses, and demonstrations involving embalming fluids?

Our usual headquarters was the historic Menger Hotel in San Antonio, right next to the Alamo. On paper, it sounded impressive. The hotel had history, character, and an indoor pool that felt like pure luxury when you were a kid. There was also a parrot in the lobby who had picked up a vocabulary that probably came from a long line of traveling funeral directors—and he wasn't shy about sharing it.

But let's be honest. Funeral conventions were not Disneyland.

When we weren't swimming or daring each other to see what new words the parrot had learned, we wandered the exhibit hall. And if you've never been to a funeral convention exhibit hall, picture a carnival—except instead of cotton candy and Ferris wheels, you've got casket vendors, vault vendors, and funeral car companies.

Every booth handed out something. Candy. Toys. Trinkets. By the end of the day, our pockets were full of junk we didn't need and sugar we probably shouldn't have had.

There was only one item we knew better than to bring home: the paddleball toy.

Sure, it was fun for about five minutes. But Mom always confiscated it before long. In her hands, it stopped being a toy and became her preferred discipline device. Somewhere along the way, the ball and rubber band would disappear, and suddenly it was just a paddle—with purpose.

By the time I had kids of my own, I decided they deserved a different kind of summer memory. By the early 1980s, we traded funeral conventions for South Padre Island.

No caskets.

No vaults.

No paddleball weapons.

Just sand, sun, and seafood.

I still owned my limousine then, which turned out to be the perfect family travel vehicle. The back was converted into a bed, and I'd load it up with movies for the kids before the long drive. Not that it mattered much, Jon only wanted to watch Ghostbusters.

Every summer, we'd leave Fort Worth at four in the morning, the kids asleep in the back, the road quiet, and the world feeling far away. By the time they woke up, we were halfway there. Those trips were about as close to perfection as life ever gets beach days, great food, no on-call duties, and best of all, no funeral homes.

Toward the end of the decade, my brother Vic came up with an idea.

Instead of South Padre, why not Rockport?

He had purchased a condo there, right on a canal that led out into the bay. It wasn't exactly a beach town, but it was on the water—and it was half the distance from Fort Worth. That alone sounded like a win.

One summer, we decided to test it out. We brought along my father-in-law, an avid fisherman, and our bass boat. Rockport had a reputation as a fishing paradise, and we were ready to see if it lived up to the billing.

We spotted an island offshore, surrounded by fishing boats. Without hesitation, Jon, my father-in-law, and I took off toward it at full speed.

Because what could possibly go wrong?

Well, it turns out Rockport isn't just a name. It's a warning.

What we didn't know—what no one thought to mention—was that there was a man-made channel boats were supposed to follow. Stray outside that channel, and you'd find barnacle-covered rocks sitting about twelve inches below the surface.

The other boats around us? Boston Whalers. Six-inch draft. Built to skim right over trouble.

Our boat? Not so much.

Rock met propeller.

Propeller lost.

We limped back to shore quieter than we left, a little humbled and significantly less confident in our nautical skills.

Standing there, looking at that damaged prop, it finally hit me.

I may have successfully escaped the funeral conventions of my childhood—but I hadn't escaped life's lessons. And apparently, one of those lessons was learning when to stay in the channel.

Both on the water…

…and everywhere else.

Chapter 22: Can I Get a Haircut

Because, naturally, when you spend your days as a funeral director, the next logical step is to open a luxury hair salon.

This adventure began when Jon's mother, Eleanor—spoiler alert: wife #1—started talking about needing a change. Eleanor had been a hairstylist for over twenty years, and she and another stylist were tired of their salon in Hurst. They wanted something better. Something newer. Something that didn't feel like the same old grind.

They weren't alone. A handful of other stylists felt the same way.

Me? I smelled opportunity.

At the time, Colleyville was just beginning to turn into what would eventually become—a magnet for people moving in from all over the country. Big houses. New money. And an ever-growing population of women with disposable income, flexible schedules, and husbands who traveled out of town Monday through Friday.

In other words, a town full of women looking for something to do.

And we were about to give them exactly that.

We didn't want to open just another salon. We wanted to create a destination. So, we went all in. Eighteen chairs, each leased to an individual stylist. Two nail stations. Five shampoo ladies. At any given time, twenty-five women worked under one roof.

And let me tell you—there was never a dull moment.

Each stylist was her own boss, setting her own hours and managing her own clients, while we handled bookings and provided flexible shampoo assistance. It worked beautifully. Everyone had independence, and the place ran like a well-oiled machine—most days.

It didn't take long for the salon to become the place to be in Colleyville.

Every time I dropped by—usually at night to help with ordering supplies or fixing whatever had broken that day—the place was buzzing.

Energy everywhere. Laughter. Stories. And a level of conversation that made it very clear I was the only man in the room.

And let's just say this: hairstylists know how to let their hair down.

Yes, pun intended.

We even hosted a few legendary pool parties over the years, which taught me something important: hairstylists are just as entertaining outside of work as they are inside. More so. With Eleanor running the salon full-time, dining out became a regular part of life, and I wasn't about to complain about that.

But here's the part I didn't see coming.

Owning a salon meant wholesale access to salon-quality beauty products.

And what does a funeral home also require?

Salon-quality beauty products.

Suddenly, Harveson & Cole had access to the best cosmetics, nail polishes, shampoos, rinses—everything you'd want if presentation mattered.

And in funeral service, presentation absolutely matters.

Our dearly departed had never looked better.

I had managed to turn a side business into an unexpected funeral home advantage, and I didn't even plan it that way. It just happened.

Call it luck.

Call it timing.

Or call it what it was—

Shear genius.

Chapter 23: Cowboys, Charity, and a Very Satisfying Redemption

If life has taught me anything, it's this: sometimes you make a spectacular mess in front of a room full of people...

And sometimes you get the chance to fix it.

I had gotten deeply involved in the Fort Worth Optimist Club. What started as an occasional luncheon became a Friday meeting I rarely missed. Before long, I wasn't just showing up; I was chairing things. Committees. Events. Eventually, the golf tournament.

Which, honestly, felt like a perfect fit.

My dad always said he was never much of a "joiner," but I knew one of us needed to be out in the community for Thompson's Harveson & Cole. Besides Optimist, I was also serving on the board of the Arthritis Foundation, helping organize their annual charity golf tournament alongside another rather legendary baseball man—Bobby Bragan.

If you ever needed someone to work a room, Bobby was your guy. Funny. Sharp. Quick with a story. Every civic club in town had him on speed dial because he could turn a polite lunch into a standing ovation.

By my second year working with Bobby, the Arthritis Foundation tournament was thriving. We brought in close to $100,000 a year and spent nearly all of it on prizes, players, and the celebrities Bobby attracted. It was one of the biggest charity golf events in the area.

One year, I played in that tournament with Eddie Robinson.

If you grew up loving baseball, you knew Eddie. Former Major League player. Later, General Manager of the Texas Rangers. Scout. Gentleman. And a man with a huge heart.

Somewhere between shots, Eddie looked at me and said,

"You know, we've got a lot of Major League Baseball alumni living around here. It'd be great if we could do a tournament with them and a local charity."

That was Eddie in a nutshell.

He was heavily involved in the Major League Baseball Players' Alumni Association, and he knew the truth most people didn't see. Today's players make millions and have pensions. Eddie's generation didn't. No long-term contracts. No safety net.

Some of his old teammates were barely scraping by. A few were living in Medicaid-supported nursing homes that weren't exactly five-star resorts.

Eddie wanted to help them.

And that's when the light came on for me.

"Eddie," I said, "my Optimist Club needs a real boost for our golf tournament—and our biggest program is a Little League Baseball for underprivileged kids."

Former ball players. Disadvantaged kids. Baseball.

It was a perfect match.

We took the idea to the MLBPAA headquarters in St. Pete Beach, Florida, and before long, alumni groups in other cities were launching their own tournaments. What started locally began spreading across the country.

Eventually, we had national sponsors—companies like Rolaids, American Tourister, and others—each contributing $5,000 per tournament. Before long, there were more than twenty tournaments nationwide.

To kick things off properly, Eddie wanted to bring in the executives from those companies, along with some Hall of Famers. I booked a suite at the Hilton Hotel in downtown Fort Worth and arranged a private cocktail party. We flew everyone in and put them up at the Hilton.

Everything was going beautifully.

Until my wife and I walked into the hotel around midday to set up the suite.

That's when we realized the Hilton was also hosting…

The National Gay Rodeo.

Now, we expected to see cowboys in Texas.

We just weren't expecting this variety.

These cowboys were dressed to the nines—bedazzled hats, custom chaps, boots that probably cost more than my first car—and they were not shy about their affection for one another.

To say it caught us off guard would be an understatement.

That evening's cocktail party produced some… lively conversation. Most of our guests agreed: yes, they expected cowboys in Texas. No, they didn't expect them to kiss each other in the hotel lobby.

But here's the thing—it didn't matter.

The event was a hit. The sponsors were thrilled. The tournament was set up for record-breaking success. And the momentum was real.

And that's when I decided it was time to fully redeem myself at the Optimist Club.

For the weekly luncheon kickoff, I brought in Eddie Robinson and Dr. Bobby Brown.

Now Bobby Brown wasn't just any doctor. He was a former New York Yankees player who had played alongside legends like DiMaggio and Berra—and at that time, he was President of the American League.

These were big deals.

Before the luncheon, both Eddie and Bobby told me the same thing:

"We'll take questions—but we don't want to answer a bunch of stupid ones."

So, we devised a plan.

I told the audience to write their questions down and drop them into a hat I brought. I'd draw the questions, and Eddie and Bobby would answer them.

What no one knew was that I wasn't pulling questions from the crowd at all.

I had a list.

Eddie and Bobby had approved it.

Every question was exactly what they wanted.

It was smooth. Funny. Informative. Engaging.

No decomposed bodies.

No belly dancers.

No phone calls afterward asking if I'd lost my mind.

It was—hands down—one of the best programs the Optimist Club ever had.

And for a little extra icing on the cake?

Eddie and Bobby came out to our Optimist Little League fields for Opening Day and threw out the first pitch.

These were underprivileged kids—many of whom had never seen a Major League player up close, much less met one. Watching their faces light up that day… that's the kind of moment that stays with you.

That was my quiet revenge.

Not with embarrassment. Not with apologies.

But with something that mattered.

And from that point on, whenever someone mentioned that medical examiner luncheon—or that belly dancer—I just smiled.

Because I knew how the story really ended.

With a grand slam.

Chapter 24: From Fairway to Fleeing: The Great Club Switch of '88

By the late '80s, Woodhaven was changing—and not in the "new carpet in the 9th Hole" kind of way.

It was changing in the "keep your head on a swivel and don't dawdle in the parking lot" kind of way.

One afternoon, after a round, I was walking toward my car when I noticed two young guys pulling into the lot. Now, I'm not one of those people who thinks every young person is up to no good—but this car didn't exactly scream member's kid, and these two didn't look like they were there to argue over whether a putt was "good" or not.

Call it instinct. Call it growing up in a business where you learn to read rooms fast. Either way, I got a bad feeling.

I picked up my pace, got into my car, and locked the doors.

A guy just a few cars down from me wasn't as lucky.

Before he could even react, the passenger in that car rolled down the window, stuck a gun out like he was ordering off a drive-thru menu, and robbed him right there in broad daylight.

Then they sped off as they'd just run an errand.

I bolted into the pro shop, and the victim was already telling Mike Duggar—our club pro—what had just happened. While he's describing his little near-death experience, another member bursts through the door and announces he'd just been robbed while walking off the third green.

The third green.

That's not supposed to be part of the course management plan.

And that's when it hit me: this wasn't a one-off. It was becoming a pattern.

Over the next few weeks, the stories kept coming. Cars broke into. Guys are getting mugged. People feel uneasy walking to their vehicles. The whole place had started to feel less like a country club and more like the opening scene of a crime documentary.

Now, Woodhaven has been good to me. It's where I got folded into the gangsome, met some wonderful people, and got branded "Digger" for life. I have many good memories there.

But there comes a point where even the most loyal member must admit golf is supposed to lower your blood pressure, not raise it.

A group of us finally decided, enough is enough. We needed a safer place to play, preferably one where you didn't have to look over your shoulder between shots.

Ridglea had been on my radar for a long time. Two courses. Strong membership. Great atmosphere. And most importantly… zero reports of armed robbery on the back nine.

I made the switch.

Ridglea didn't have an official gangsome like Woodhaven, but it didn't take long to find a good group of guys to play with. And as it turns out, it became more than just a safer place to hit golf balls.

Ridglea also became a great spot for funeral home receptions and dinners after services—one of those places families already knew, trusted, and felt comfortable walking into. Getting involved in committees and meeting more people didn't hurt either. It gave me one more way to stay plugged into the community, which mattered to me—and it mattered to our business.

It was a win-win.

It did come with one minor problem.

Somewhere along the way, word got out that I had once—once—worn pink shorts on a golf course.

And if you don't know anything about golf culture, know this: golfers are wonderful people… who will remember your worst wardrobe decision until the end of time.

For a moment, I was in real danger of becoming "The Pink Flamingo" all over again.

But I handled it the same way I've handled a lot of things in life: I laughed just enough to let them enjoy it, then changed the subject fast and moved on like it never happened.

Crisis averted.

Moving to Ridglea wasn't just about better golf. It was about peace of mind. Woodhaven had been a great club for years—but when your afternoon round starts feeling like you should be wearing a bulletproof vest to the parking lot, it's time to pack up your bag and go.

At Ridglea, I found new golf buddies, a good home for community events, and the simple luxury of finishing a round without wondering who might be waiting behind your car.

And honestly… that alone made the switch worth it.

Chapter 25: Some of the Best

Thompson's Harveson & Cole has always been home to a colorful cast of characters.

Some people came and went. Others stayed thirty, forty, even fifty years—so long that they felt less like employees and more like part of the building itself. If you asked anyone who ever worked at THC to name the most memorable personalities, you'd get a long list, each name followed by a story.

There was Leo, whose loyalty ran so deep that his entire family felt like part of the company.

Ed had a sense of humor that surfaced at exactly the wrong moment—and somehow made it the right one.

Burt worked for us for more than forty years and was a complete ghost outside of work. No one ever saw his house. No one socialized with him. He arrived, did his job flawlessly, and disappeared.

Frank was our front-desk man, a retired Channel 5 anchorman who had once broadcast one of the station's first live events. By the time he was buzzing me on the intercom, that smooth broadcast voice was long gone.

And then there was Roger—the birdman—who never said no to me, my sister, or my dad, no matter what the request was.

They were the fabric of the place. THC wasn't just a funeral home; it was a collection of loyalty, work ethic, and more than a few odd habits that somehow all worked together.

One random day in 1988, Frank buzzed me from the front desk.

"There's a girl up here looking for a funeral director job."

That alone got my attention. At the time, women in funeral service were still rare. A woman walking in cold, off the street, asking for a job? That was almost unheard of.

I went up to the front and met a young woman with quiet intensity. She didn't waste time. She told me her story, and within minutes, I was floored.

She had grown up dirt poor in El Paso. Hitchhiked to Dallas just to attend the newly renamed Dallas Institute of Funeral Service—DIFS. Her family support plan fell apart, leaving her sleeping wherever she could. Eventually, another student took her in, just long enough for her to finish school. Despite everything stacked against her, she excelled.

Now she had her diploma—and nowhere to go.

Every funeral home in Dallas and Fort Worth had turned her down.

THC was her last stop before hitchhiking back to El Paso.

As luck would have it, we were looking for an apprentice. And after hearing her story, I felt that unmistakable gut punch that tells you, this matters.

I told her to wait and went straight to my brother, Vic.

"I found someone for the job," I said.

"Hire him," Vic replied without looking up.

"Well… " It's actually a her," I said.

That got his attention.

Not only was she a woman, but she was also Hispanic—something we had never had before. Vic hesitated, but he wasn't someone who ignored talent when it was staring at him in the face.

"Just meet her," I said.

He did. And like me, he was moved.

There was only one hurdle left—Dad.

Vic and I went to him together.

"Dad, we've got a great candidate for the apprentice position."

"Hire him," Dad said.

"Actually, Dad, it's a her."

He raised an eyebrow.

We told him her story. How every other funeral home had turned her away. How determined she was. How hard she had worked just to get in the door.

Dad listened quietly. Then he nodded.

"Hire her."

That day, Sylvia became part of THC.

Over the next twenty-plus years, she became one of Dad's all-time favorite hires. Her story became one we often told, especially when people asked how she got her start.

It was a reminder that the best people don't always come with polished résumés or perfect timing.

Sometimes, they walk in off the street with nothing but grit, determination, and a story that deserves a chance.

And sometimes, if you're lucky, you recognize it when it's standing right in front of you.

Moments like that make you think you've got things figured out.

That's usually when the phone rings.

Chapter 26: April Fools and Divorce Blues

That morning started like any other birthday.

Maybe a few phone calls. A joke or two about getting older. The usual rhythm of work at the funeral home. Nothing dramatic. Nothing memorable.

Then the phone rang.

On the other end was a man whose voice I recognized.

"Mr. Thompson, you took care of my mom a few months ago. I need to serve you some papers, and I don't want to embarrass you in front of anyone. Could we do this in private?"

I paused.

Serve me some papers?

Not. embarrass me?

My mind ran through the list of possibilities, none of which landed anywhere near the truth. Before I could overthink it, I told him to meet me at my office behind the funeral home.

A few minutes later, he arrived—papers in hand.

I opened the envelope, skimmed the first page, and felt that strange, familiar sensation that only comes when life decides to show its sense of humor.

Divorce papers.

On my birthday.

Delivered by a man whose family I had helped just months earlier.

He looked genuinely uncomfortable. "I'm really sorry about this," he said, as if that might soften the moment.

I nodded, let out a small laugh—because what else can you do? — and said, "Well, at least I won't forget the anniversary of this one."

Happy birthday to me.

Sometimes life doesn't whisper when it's time for a change.

Sometimes it hands you papers… and makes sure the date sticks.

Funny thing about starting over—you don't usually know you're doing it at the time. You just keep showing up, going to the places you've always gone, talking to the people you've always talked to, assuming life will settle down when it's ready. I had no idea that just a few weeks later, standing over the 18th hole at Colonial, it was about to do exactly that.

Chapter 27: Honeymoon Surprises

One of the must-attend events in Fort Worth every year is the Colonial National Invitational Golf Tournament. It's part tradition, part social calendar, and part reunion. You're just as likely to run into an old friend as you are to brush shoulders with a golf legend.

Wednesday is Pro-Am Day, and if you want to be right in the middle of everything, you go straight to the Terrace Room above the 18th hole. It's always packed wall to wall—people talking over one another, drinks flowing, the kind of energy you only get when everyone knows this is exactly where they're supposed to be.

That's where my life changed again.

I was newly single, still getting used to the idea that my marriage was officially over, and not exactly on the hunt for anything serious. Then I met Janice.

We talked. We laughed. We exchanged numbers. A few days later, I called her. When she answered, she said, "My friend and I joked it would be the undertaker who called first."

I wasn't sure if that was a compliment or a warning, but either way, I figured I was off to a decent start.

One date turned into another. Then another. She was beautiful, successful, sharp, and had a great sense of humor. I'd love to tell you she fell for me immediately, but the real test came with her dogs. Fortunately, they didn't try to bite me, which I took as a very good sign.

By September, my divorce was final. Janice and I were having lunch one day when, in what can only be described as a remarkably unromantic proposal, I said, "You know we're probably going to get married, so we may as well do it."

Smooth, I know.

To my surprise, she agreed. Her only condition was simple: "It should be before Thanksgiving or after New Year's."

We chose before Thanksgiving.

We wanted something small, intimate, and simple—a short and sweet ceremony in the chapel at First Presbyterian Church, with Dr. Bohl, a good friend, officiating. What we didn't plan on was everyone showing up. When we arrived, the chapel was full, and people were standing outside.

Dr. Bohl loved an audience, and he rose to the occasion. Our short service ran a little longer than planned, but it was perfect. On November 14, 1992, Janice said, "I do," and I became a very lucky man.

Because we put the wedding together quickly, we didn't have many honeymoon options. We booked a cruise out of San Juan, stopping in Aruba, Curaçao, Virgin Gorda, and St. Thomas before heading back.

When we saw the ship, reality set in. It was old. It was small. And it looked like it should have been retired a years earlier. Our cabin was so small you almost had to step outside to change your mind.

But it was our honeymoon. We decided to make the best of it.

On the first night after dinner, we wandered into bingo—not exactly what I had envisioned for a honeymoon evening, but why not? The last game of the night was blackout bingo, with a jackpot of a thousand dollars.

I won.

That win led directly to my next questionable decision.

They were auctioning off five wooden horses for a horse race scheduled on the last night of the cruise. The owners would name their horse, deck it out, and spend the week convincing other passengers to bet on it. Since I'd just won a thousand bucks, I bought one.

We named him Big Tex.

Janice is a proud University of Texas alum, so Big Tex was painted burnt orange and decorated accordingly. He became an instant favorite. By midweek, we couldn't walk into a bar without our drinks already waiting. We made friends all over the ship, and the crew treated us like royalty.

On the last night, the betting odds were posted. Big Tex was the favorite, which meant the payout was terrible.

So naturally, I bet on another horse.

Big Tex lost. So did the bet on another horse.

But by then, it didn't matter. We had a great time, met wonderful people, and added several places to our list of destinations we'd return to—which we did.

It may not have been a luxury cruise, and I may have managed to bet against myself and lose, but it was our honeymoon.

And nothing was going to put a damper on that.

Chapter 28: Farm Life and Cosmic Consequences

Janice's parents lived on what they called a farm, but that term was somewhat misleading. They didn't actually farm anything, at least not in the traditional sense. What they really had were two sprawling properties.

The main place held a house, wide pastures, two ponds, a hay barn, an outbuilding with workout equipment, and another shed full of farm tools. The second property was mostly pasture and trees, also with two ponds—perfect for cows to wade in and city folks like me to stand around admiring.

Before we headed out there for the first time, Janice gave me a gentle warning.

"They might look at you a little funny."

Then she explained why.

Years earlier, Janice's little brother, John Martin Furry, had passed away when he was about the same age Jon was now.. And now here she was, bringing home a Jon and a Martin.

If that doesn't make you pause and wonder whether the universe enjoys a good inside joke, nothing will.

Still, if first impressions were an Olympic sport, Myrl and Fawn Furry would've taken home the gold for kindness. They were two of the warmest, most gracious people I had ever met. Don't let that fool you, though—Myrl was sharp as a tack. He ran a cow–calf operation and his own oil and gas production company.

Almost immediately, he handed Jon and me an invitation we couldn't refuse.

"Hop in the truck, boys. Let's take a ride."

And just like that, we were off.

Now, growing up in Texas doesn't automatically mean you know how to work at a ranch. People like to think we all rode horses to school and roped cattle between math class and lunch. The truth is, I grew up in Fort Worth—a city boy through and through.

But there I was, riding shotgun while Myrl checked cows, threw hay, fixed fences, and stopped by oil leases like it was just another afternoon. It didn't take long for me to realize I needed a good pair of leather gloves—this was real work.

Jon had his own discoveries. At one point, standing near a pump jack, he wrinkled his nose and complained about the smell.

Myrl just smiled.

"No, Jon. This smells really good."

Only an oil man could say that with a straight face.

Those truck rides became our time. Myrl and I talked about everything. He told me about growing up dirt poor in a tiny Texas town called Grovesnor, north of Brownwood. Later, he took me there. The town was basically abandoned—empty buildings, quiet roads, nothing left but memories.

He also shared stories from World War II. When the Army drafted him, they put him on a train full of recruits and sent them zigzagging across Texas for an entire day—only for him to end up in Abilene, barely a hundred miles from where he started. A long trip to go nowhere.

After boot camp, he shipped out to England to prepare for D-Day. To avoid seasickness, he stayed on deck the entire crossing. Originally assigned clerical work because of his education, Myrl volunteered for infantry duty as D-Day approached—a decision he later admitted he regretted during the Battle of the Bulge.

My mother-in-law, Fawn, grew up even poorer than Myrl, in a place called Cross Cut. After raising her family, she returned to school and became a teacher, a role she loved and held for years. She was small in stature but strong in every way that mattered. Quiet, steady, and the glue that held everything together.

Despite everything they'd been through, Myrl and Fawn never lost their love for baseball, especially the Texas Rangers. It became our daily ritual to call each other during games, either to celebrate a great play or complain loudly about a bad one.

Thanks to my friendship with Eddie Robinson and our work with the Major League Baseball Players' Alumni Association, I even got to take Myrl along to meet some of his baseball heroes. Watching him light up in those moments was something I'll never forget.

From that very first visit, Myrl and Fawn took Jon and me in as their own. No hesitation. No conditions. Just family.

And for that—for all of it—I will always be grateful.

Chapter 29: Scouting Shenanigans

Possum Bears and Cold Showers

After the wedding, life settled into something that felt wonderfully normal.

Janice and I were married, we were living in the TCU area, and one of the greatest gifts that came with it was having Jon move in with us. Before long, it was clear we needed to get him settled into a school that challenged him academically and provided opportunities to burn off energy.

We enrolled him at Hill School—a fantastic place that checked all the boxes. On his very first day, Jon made friends and quickly proved something I had suspected but hadn't fully appreciated yet: the kid was an athlete. Basketball, baseball, and football, if there was a ball involved, he could play it. I'd love to take credit for that, but since my own athletic peak was being a kickball champion in elementary school, we'll just call it natural talent.

As much as I loved watching him play sports, I had another idea for father-son bonding.

Cub Scouts.

I loved scouting when I was a kid, and convincing Jon to join was really my excuse to relive my glory days. I still knew all the best camping spots—or at least I thought I did—so we booked trips to the same places I had camped years earlier. That summer, we signed up for the big camp at Leonard Scout Campground.

That's where my nostalgia ran headfirst into reality.

The plan was solid. Three other dads had agreed to be chaperones for the weekend. Everything was lined up. Then, parents started dropping their kids off.

One by one, each of the three dads pulled me aside with the same guilty look and the same line:

"I'm really sorry, but something came up, and I can't stay."

And just like that, I was the lone adult responsible for twelve eight-year-olds.

In the pitch-black woods.

With kids who had never been away from home before.

This was not in the brochure.

I did my best to keep things under control. First order of business: survival. I set up a chair in the middle of our tent circle, flashlight in hand, ready to fight off wild animals, homesickness, or whatever else the night decided to throw at me.

Before lights out, I gave one very clear instruction:

"Do not keep food in your tents. The possums out here have a major sweet tooth."

For a while, things were quiet. Then, around 2 a.m., the screaming started.

One tent exploded with panic.

"THERE'S A BEAR INSIDE!"

Now, I had already seen their so-called bear leaving the tent earlier, and unless bears had recently shrunk to the size of a housecat and grown a long, rat-like tail, this was a possum.

That logic didn't help the kids.

So, I did what any rational scout leader would do in that situation. I told them to cough up every piece of candy and every snack they had. Out came half-melted chocolate bars, sticky gum, and partially eaten bags of Skittles. I gathered it all up and tossed it far, far away from camp.

Possum crisis averted.

The next morning, I was reminded of one very important thing I had completely forgotten about scout camps.

There is no warm running water.

The showers weren't just cold, they felt like punishment. By day three, I was convinced I had somehow offended the spirits of scouting past, and this was their way of humbling me.

I toughed it out. We made it through the week. And when it was over, Jon and I came to the same conclusion.

Scouting just wasn't our thing.

Though, honestly, I wouldn't have minded sticking with it a little longer—

As long as someone else handled possum patrol.

While home life was full of possums, cold showers, and eight-year-old chaos, work was an entirely different world.

Chapter 30: Funeral Home Adventures

Life was good.

The funeral home was thriving. Dad, Vic, and I were working together regularly—meeting with families, running services, and keeping Thompson's Harveson & Cole operating like a well-oiled machine. Janice and I traveled often, making a point of taking at least two trips a year, one domestic and one international. We had a great group of friends, some of whom even joined us along the way.

After years of playing musical golf clubs, I finally landed where I'd wanted to be all along and joined River Crest. Jon excelled in school, both academically and athletically, earning Athlete of the Year honors twice.

Everything was running smoothly.

And then came a call I'll never forget.

Dad was up in Syracuse on his annual buying trip. Vic was down at his place in Rockport. That meant I was manning the fort.

At 5:30 a.m., the funeral home phone rang. The family name was one I knew well. I went to the hospital with one of our staff members, where the deceased's son was already waiting. He was gracious, well-spoken, and calm—remarkably so, considering the circumstances.

We talked for a while. Then I asked the usual question.

"Would you like us to bring our cot in to receive your mother?"

He paused and said, "Can I help?"

That wasn't a common request. But something about the way he asked made me nod.

"Sure."

As we placed his mother on the cot, I noticed something. He wasn't ready to let go. He walked with us to the elevator. Then out to the car. Then he followed us all the way back to the funeral home.

Along the way, he kept saying the same thing.

"I just can't imagine seeing my mother in a casket."

After enough years in funeral service, you learn when to listen—and when to rethink the script.

I stopped and said, "If that would be difficult for you, we could place her in a bed for the viewing."

His face changed instantly.

"Could we?"

"Of course."

He hesitated, then asked one more thing.

"Could we use her actual bed?"

It wasn't a typical request.

But again, I nodded.

"Absolutely."

And just like that, a routine arrangement became something entirely different.

Over the next few days, we transformed one of our visitation rooms into a perfect recreation of her bedroom. The bed. The nightstand. The chairs. The bric-a-brac. Every detail was placed exactly where it belonged.

That was only the beginning.

The family chose a Saturday night service at Broadway Baptist—because Saturday night was prime time for the son. So, we pulled out every stop.

A two-hundred-piece orchestra, made up of first-chair strings from the Fort Worth, Dallas, Houston, and Austin symphonies.

A choir of more than two hundred voices.

Music commissioned specifically for the service.

Eighteen limousines, each assigned with a detailed car list.

Floral arrangements, unlike anything I had ever seen.

Dad cut his trip short and flew home.

On the night of the service, all eighteen limousines were staged at the funeral home. Every available Fort Worth motor officer was there, along with five more we had hired. From the home to the church, and back again, the procession was something to behold.

Then came the eulogy.

Delivered by Paul Harvey.

Yes. That Paul Harvey.

The church was filled with dignitaries from across the country. The orchestra was flawless. The choir was magnificent. Every detail unfolded exactly as planned.

It was, without question, one of the most elaborate services I have ever been part of.

At the end, ten hired pallbearers carried out a three-inch plank mahogany Marcellus Masterpiece casket.

I drove the son and his closest friends.

After a few quiet moments, I asked him, "Was everything as you hoped?"

He looked out the window for a long moment. Then he turned to me, smiled, and said something I'll never forget.

"That service was perfect. It wasn't ostentatious at all."

I almost laughed.

Two hundred musicians.

Eighteen limousines.

A church full of dignitaries.

Paul Harvey delivering the eulogy.

Not ostentatious at all.

But at that moment, I understood.

To him, it wasn't excess.

It was simply what his mother deserved.

And in the end, that's all that really mattered.

Chapter 31: Vic's Last Laugh

It was mid-December of 1994 when Vic started having serious health issues.

Vic was larger than life—the kind of guy everyone loved, admired, and never forgot. He was my older brother, my idol, and one of the funniest, most charismatic people I've ever known. Even now, thirty years later, people still come up to me and tell Vic stories, their faces lighting up as if he had just walked into the room.

He and his wife, Carla, married immediately after graduating from Texas Wesleyan, where she also attended. They had three incredible boys—Theo, Tim, and Trent—who have grown into outstanding men, each carrying a piece of their father's warmth, humor, and kindness.

At first, Vic brushed off how he was feeling. He still came to work, but something wasn't right. On Monday, he called in sick. On Tuesday, he called in again. By Thursday, Dad got worried—and Dad wasn't the type to panic.

Before funeral service, Dad had been a Chief Pharmacist's Mate in the Navy. He'd seen everything, treated everything, and very little rattled him. But this time, something did.

Dad went to check on Vic, and being ever practical, suggested he go to the hospital for an IV. By Friday, Vic seemed better. He was cracking jokes, entertaining a steady stream of visitors, and acting like his usual self. We all breathed a little easier. Maybe it was just a bad case of the flu after all.

Saturday, December 18th, my mother was carrying on one of her long-standing Christmas traditions—taking the grandkids to see a holiday movie—when my brother Tim, a priest, walked into the theater.

"Thompson family," he said quietly. "Come out to the lobby."

The moment we saw his face, we knew.

Tim told us Vic had taken a turn for the worse and that we needed to get to the hospital immediately. We rushed to All Saints, where they had set up a family room for us.

When the doctor came in, his face said it all.

"His system is shutting down."

Just the day before, Vic had been laughing and joking. Now we were being told there was nothing more to be done. One by one, we went in to say goodbye.

That night, around 2 a.m., Vic passed away.

One week before Christmas.

And suddenly, we were planning a funeral we never wanted to plan.

I had always assumed that Dad—the man who had spent his life comforting grieving families—would be stoic, steady, unshakable. And I thought Mom—deeply faithful, always praying her rosary—would grieve openly and visibly.

Grief, it turns out, doesn't follow expectations.

Dad grieved openly. Far more than I ever imagined. And Mom, who had always worn her heart on her sleeve, showed almost no emotion at all.

Over time, their grief took very different paths.

Dad talked about Vic. He shared stories, laughed about the past, and allowed himself to fully remember his son. He grieved—and eventually, he celebrated him.

Mom never spoke Vic's name again. If someone mentioned him, she quietly left the room. She never cried in front of us. She never reminisced. She carried it all inside. I truly believe she silently grieved Vic's loss for the rest of her life.

Even in death, Vic had a way of bringing people together.

At his funeral, the chapel was filled with friends, colleagues, and family. Stories were told. Laughter broke through tears. It was all very Vic.

That was his gift—to make people feel like they belonged, like they mattered.

And that gift never faded.

I miss you, Vic.

Even now, all these years later.

I miss your humor.

I miss your wisdom.

I miss your presence.

But more than anything, I miss my big brother.

Chapter 32: The Turning Point

The mood in our family shifted the way a storm rolls in—slow at first, almost unnoticed, and then suddenly impossible to ignore.

Grief didn't just touch us. It settled in. It changed the air. And in a family business, where personal and professional lives are already tightly woven together, it felt like we were trying to keep a ship afloat in rough seas—with no captain.

Looking back now, I realize something that took me years to admit.

Just like my mother, I never really allowed myself the time or space to grieve.

Instead, I did what so many of us do when the world keeps moving, whether we're ready or not. I put my head down and kept going. We all did. We showed up. We did our jobs. We tried to act normal.

But nothing was normal.

And the business felt it.

The steady rhythm that had always defined Harveson & Cole was gone. Things still functioned, but the cadence was off. The confidence wasn't there. The feeling—the one you can't quantify but everyone senses—had changed.

Longtime employees, people who had been with us for decades, started leaving. Some retired. Some moved on. Some just needed a fresh start.

Honestly, I couldn't blame them.

The foundation we had built over so many years suddenly felt unsteady, and I began to wonder if I was holding on too tightly to something that no longer fit the way it once had.

By 1998, I had been at Harveson & Cole for twenty-two years.

And deep in my gut, I knew something I didn't yet know how to say out loud.

It was time.

Not because I didn't care.

Not because I was running from anything.

But because I was done trying to force things back into a shape they no longer wanted to take.

That chapter was closing.

And for the first time, instead of fighting it, I was finally willing to turn the page—and see what came next.

Chapter 33: From Tee Time to Funeral Home

At forty, I had a realization that caught me completely off guard.

After a lifetime of working—or, if we're being honest, hanging around—Thompson's Harveson & Cole, I was officially unemployed and directionless. For the first time in my adult life, I had to ask myself a question I'd never really had to answer before.

What now?

At first, the answer was easy.

Golf.

Life was sweet. I was playing in the gangsome at River Crest, living what I considered a perfectly respectable post-career lifestyle. Every morning, my wife would ask, "What are you going to do today?"

"I'm going to play in the gangsome," I'd say.

And I meant it.

Then came the lists.

"Before you go, could you do this?"

Which became, "This and that."

Which eventually turned into "this, that, and every damn thing."

When my pre-golf to-do list started cutting into my tee time, I knew the honeymoon phase was over. It was time to get a job.

The problem was—I'd sold my interest in the funeral home. And attached to that sale was a non-compete clause that was wrapped around Loop 820 like a noose. If I wanted to open my own place, I had to go beyond the loop.

About that time, I heard a rumor: the most successful funeral home in Weatherford was about to be sold to SCI, the corporate funeral home behemoth.

Competing with a corporate operation? Easy. They're overpriced and under-serve. I figured I'd have the market locked up in no time.

A few days later, my friend Roger Williams invited me to lunch and a tour of some properties in Weatherford. Just as I was picturing my grand Weatherford takeover, the truth came out.

The rumor was just that—a rumor.

The funeral home wasn't selling after all. And competing head-to-head with a well-run, family-owned funeral home wasn't my style. So, it was back to square one.

That night, I turned to Janice and said, "It's time to hit the mid-cities."

The next day, I started driving. Keller. Southlake. Colleyville. And finally, Grapevine.

Late in the afternoon, I called Janice and said, "It's got to be Grapevine. This town has charm, great properties, and the right feel. Tomorrow, I'm calling our realtor."

As I was saying that, I pulled up in front of a three-story Victorian house built in 1888, with a For Lease sign out front.

I stopped the car.

"I just found our funeral home," I said.

"What?" she replied—reasonably.

"I'm standing in front of it. Let me call you back."

The house was known as the Dorris House, and I knew almost immediately it was the one. The next day, Janice and I toured it, and before long, we had a contract.

The outside needed only minor cosmetic work. The inside, on the other hand, needed… everything.

Dad's funeral home was just as old and always immaculate, so I knew what was possible. I hired an interior decorator, a contractor, and jumped headfirst into renovation mode. The walls had more cracks than a plumber's convention, but I wasn't deterred.

I even found a piece of the original 1888 wallpaper in a second-floor closet and had the pattern recreated. Then I took it to a fabric store to match drapes and wall coverings.

I spent months combing antique stores for period-appropriate furniture—only to learn that Victorian people were apparently much smaller and far less padded than modern humans. Comfort was clearly not their priority.

Somewhere during all of this, things got a little... strange.

One night, I was working late on the third floor, which I planned to use as my office—and occasionally, a bedroom. The phone system had a speaker feature that activated a dial tone when pressed. A spiral staircase connected all three floors, so sound carried easily.

Suddenly, I heard the dial tone.

Not from my phone.

From downstairs.

I went down and turned it off, assuming my contractor was playing a prank. But his truck was gone. I went back upstairs.

A few minutes later, it happened again.

By the third time, every hair on my body was standing at attention. I don't know if I believe in ghosts—but if they exist, this one clearly had opinions about long-distance calls.

Anyway, back to the renovations.

The Sunday before our grand opening, the Grapevine Sun ran a feature story on the new funeral home. They interviewed longtime mayor William D. Tate and asked what he thought about the Dorris House becoming Martin Thompson Funeral Home.

His answer?

"Grapevine already has two funeral homes that have been here for over a hundred years. I don't think Grapevine needs another one. I wish the Dorris House had stayed a restaurant."

I looked at Janice and said, "Well, I don't think I'm getting a key to the city anytime soon."

And just like that, I was back in the funeral business—whether Grapevine wanted me or not.

Chapter 34: From Remodel to Roll Call: The Grapevine Gamble

Turning the Dorris House into a funeral home was a leap of faith. We'd poured ourselves into the remodel, and by December 1998, the place finally looked like what it was supposed to be: warm, polished, and ready.

Now all we needed was permission to open the doors.

I called the Texas Funeral Service Commission to schedule an inspection.

"We can get to you in about a month."

A month. Sure. Why not?

I was already opening a funeral home in a town where no one knew me, in a city with two funeral homes that had been there since the dawn of time—at least according to the mayor—so waiting another month felt about right.

The truth was, the only time I'd ever set foot in Grapevine before this was to play golf. I didn't have the advantage of a long family history as I did at Thompson's Harveson & Cole. No built-in reputation. No deep roots. No steady stream of word-of-mouth referrals.

Which meant I had to do something THC never did.

I had to advertise.

The only problem was that the remodel had eaten up my budget. I had no money for billboards, newspaper ads, or anything that required a checkbook. So, I became the advertising.

I made what I called a "book" titled Everything You Ever Wanted to Know About Funeral Service but Were Afraid to Ask.

It was a glorified spiral-bound binder from Kinko's.

But I was proud of it.

Inside, I laid out the way corporate funeral homes worked—pricing tricks, upsells, pressure tactics, the whole deal. If The American Way of Death was the big national expose, mine was the local Texas version—written with a little righteous indignation and a lot of personal experience.

My plan was simple: to get in front of pastors.

If I could meet one pastor a day, I figured word would spread. The only flaw in my plan was that I launched it in December—right when every pastor in North Texas is buried under nativity scenes, choir rehearsals, and Christmas Eve services.

I met a few, but most weren't exactly eager to sit down and talk about funerals during the holiday season. Not that I blamed them.

Then, in early January, a man in a suit walked through the front door.

"I'm with the Texas Funeral Service Commission," he said. "I'm here for your inspection."

Finally.

Thirty minutes later, he handed me a single sheet of paper—almost as thrilling as the day I got my funeral director's license.

"You're open."

Just like that, Martin Thompson Funeral Home was officially in business.

Only problem?

No one knew it.

That night, the phone rang.

It was one of the pastors I'd visited.

"Mr. Thompson, we've had a death in our congregation. I'm at the family home right now and wanted to see if you were open yet."

I made the call that night, met with the family the next day, and three days later, we conducted our first funeral.

Sometimes God gives you a little wink—just enough to keep you moving.

Ten days later, another call.

Ten days after that, another.

One funeral every ten days wasn't exactly a fast track to success—but it was a start.

And for a brand-new funeral home in a town where nobody knew my name?

That felt like the gamble had officially begun.

Chapter 35: Candice: The Worldly One

So far, I've written extensively about my son, Jon, and about many of the people who shaped my life. But there is someone missing—and that absence is intentional, not accidental.

That person is my daughter, Candice.

The truth is that our relationship has had its ups and downs. If I could go back, I'd do some things differently. Still, Candice has lived an extraordinary life, and her story belongs here alongside the rest of our family.

By 2001, Martin Thompson Funeral Home in Grapevine was beginning to find its footing. I was active in the Chamber of Commerce, Rotary, Grapevine AMBUCS, and the Grapevine–Colleyville School Foundation. I was busy and involved, yet still managed to sneak in some pretty good golf. Life felt full and steady.

Then came a phone call that changed everything.

It was September 10, 2001. I was driving back from a graveside service in Wichita Falls when Candice called. She had recently moved to New York City with a friend after graduating from my alma mater, Texas Wesleyan—yes, she followed me to "Teeny Weeny."

Candice had always been drawn to the world beyond Texas. She loved Spanish so much that she made it her major, immersing herself in the language far beyond the Tex-Mex version most of us know. She spent two semesters in Cuernavaca, Mexico, at Monterrey University, then her final semester in Barcelona, fully immersed in Castilian Spanish. By the time she graduated, North Richland Hills just wasn't going to cut it. She needed more. She needed the world.

That summer, she and her friend packed their belongings into a shared moving van and headed east, planning to find an apartment once they arrived. On September 10, Candice called to tell me they had finally found one: a one-room apartment on Madison Avenue for $2,700 a month.

Yes. You read that right.

The landlord requested that I cosign the lease. My first response was immediate.

"Candice, you don't even have a job."

She told me she had an interview the next morning with Merrill Lynch, located in Building 7 of the World Trade Center. We negotiated, argued, and eventually reached a compromise: if she got the job and her friend's parents cosigned for half, I would sign the rest.

The next morning, I was in the shower when Janice came running in.

"I think you'd better come see this."

I dried off and walked into the kitchen, where Good Morning America was showing smoke pouring from a gaping hole in the World Trade Center. They were speculating—an accident, maybe a small plane.

I tried to call Candice.

Nothing.

For what felt like an eternity, the phones were dead.

Then the phone rang.

It was Candice. She hadn't left for her interview yet. She had already spoken with the woman she was scheduled to meet, who suggested rescheduling later that afternoon. As we were talking, the second plane hit.

This wasn't an accident.

This was an attack.

I begged her to come home. She insisted she was okay, staying with friends in Midtown, and that she would check back with Merrill Lynch later. But by the end of the day, building 7 collapsed along with Towers One and Two. The interview would never happen. Merrill Lynch—like so many companies—was displaced, scattered, and forever changed.

Candice never got that interview.

Instead, she stayed.

Stubborn. Determined. Maybe a little of both.

She found work at a bar in the theater district called Faces and Names. Officially, her shift ended at 4 a.m., but in true New York fashion, the bar didn't close until the last customer left. Many mornings, Candice worked until sunrise.

A few years later, she moved to Washington, D.C., eventually landing a great job that later brought her back home.

Looking back now, I see things more clearly.

When Eleanor and I divorced, Jon came to live with me, while Candice remained closer to her mother. My bond with Jon grew strong, and Candice's bond with her mom remained equally strong. Life and circumstances pulled us in different directions.

And so today, we don't have the relationship I wish we did.

But if there's one thing life has taught me, it's that people—and relationships—have a way of circling back. In my heart, I still hope Candice and I find that path.

The week after 9/11 was strange in Grapevine. My funeral home sat at the end of a runway at DFW International Airport, and suddenly the skies were silent. I hadn't realized how constant the low rumble of airplanes had become until it was gone. The quiet felt deafening.

Everywhere you went, gas stations, restaurants—you saw stranded travelers. Hundreds of people were stuck in town, desperate to rent a car, a ride, or a way home. Many had little money. Locals did what they could, buying meals, offering rides, and helping wherever possible.

If that was what we were experiencing in Grapevine, I can only imagine what Candice experienced in New York.

Not only had her plans been erased in an instant, but she and her friends went down to the site itself—to volunteer, to see with their own eyes what had happened. Later, she told me how deeply it shook her. I believe it changed her.

It changéd all of us.

It was a moment that altered lives, redirected paths, and left scars we still carry.

And I pray we will never see another day like it again.

Some stories don't end on the page. I still believe this one doesn't have its final chapter yet.

Chapter 36: From Unknown to Unstoppable: Conquering Grapevine

When I opened Martin Thompson Funeral Home, I wanted it to be the Thompson's Harveson & Cole of Grapevine—from the service to the ambiance, from the staffing to the pricing. Every detail mattered. If I was going to do this, I was going to do it right.

There was just one small problem.

Volume.

At THC, Dad handled five hundred calls a year. That kind of volume supports a large, full-time staff without batting an eye. At forty or fifty calls a year? Not so much. So, if this place was going to survive, I had to get smart—and fast.

One of Dad's oldest friends, Kent Adair, a retired funeral director who had owned a very successful funeral home in California, began volunteering at Martin Thompson Funeral Home. Without Kent, I honestly don't know where I'd be. He brought experience, perspective, and calm when I needed all three.

Together, we took a hard look at operations and found some obvious places to cut without sacrificing service:

A 5:00 p.m. to 9:00 p.m. shift? Pointless if the phone wasn't ringing. Gone.

Sunday staffing? Not needed unless we have services. Cut.

Saturdays? Half-day if we weren't busy.

An apprentice position? Unnecessary when I was already working from 7:00 a.m. until late every night—for free.

By trimming overhead rather than cutting corners, we kept service quality high while giving the business a fighting chance to breathe.

That summer, after handling a funeral for a well-known Grapevine lady, I decided to attend the monthly Chamber of Commerce luncheon.

I walked in alone, found an empty seat at a table, and sat down completely unnoticed.

Then I heard a voice.

"I didn't know you were a Chamber member."

I turned and saw Edie Gillette, a powerhouse of a woman who seemed to know everyone in town.

"I've actually been to every luncheon since I joined," I told her.

She shook her head and smirked. "Coming to a monthly luncheon isn't being a Chamber member. You have to get involved."

And just like that, Edie took me under her wing.

She registered me as a Chamber Ambassador, an organization that greets every new business in the community. Ribbon cuttings were happening constantly, and I was at every single one. It didn't take long for people to stop asking who I was and start greeting me by name.

From there, Edie pulled me into Rotary, where I met Phil Cloud—a man with the best nickname in town long before it meant something else: Puff Daddy. Phil introduced me to Ambucs, a civic club dedicated to giving back to the community. It was full of guys like me—fun-loving, hardworking, and serious about making a difference.

Suddenly, I wasn't just in Grapevine.

I was becoming part of Grapevine.

Between Rotary luncheons, Chamber luncheons, Ambuc luncheons, and committee meetings, I never had to buy lunch again. More importantly, the phone started ringing.

People don't choose a funeral home because of a billboard or an advertisement. They choose one because they trust you. By showing up at luncheons, ribbon cuttings, committee meetings, and charity events, I became the funeral director people knew and trusted.

At the same time, Grapevine's two longtime funeral homes—Foust and Lucas—had both been swallowed up by large corporations. The problem with corporate ownership was obvious:

No full-time funeral director on staff

No presence in the Chamber, Rotary, or Ambucs

No connection to local churches

No real community involvement

They were out of touch, overpriced, and impersonal.

And that's how I won.

By cutting costs, lowering prices, and embedding myself into the community, Martin Thompson Funeral Home didn't just compete—we dominated. It didn't take long before more than eighty percent of the funeral business in Grapevine was coming through my doors.

Not bad for a guy who started out knowing absolutely no one in town.

But the truth is, this success didn't happen because of spreadsheets or staffing models alone. It happened because I stopped trying to run a funeral home from behind a desk and started showing up where people lived their lives.

And that realization changed more than just my business.

It changed me.

Chapter 37: From Joiner to Country Undertaker

My dad always prided himself on not being a "joiner."

Sure, he belonged to the Knights of Columbus and paid his dues to the Serra Club, but he never saw the point in chambers, Rotary, or civic clubs. Dad worked. Period. That had always been enough for him—and for a long time, it was enough for our family business, too.

But times had changed.

And if I wanted Martin Thompson Funeral Home to thrive in Grapevine, sitting behind my desk and waiting for the phone to ring wasn't going to cut it. I had already learned that success here wasn't about ads or signage. It was about presence.

I leaned in.

The Grapevine Chamber of Commerce became my first real proving ground. Their mission—Collaborate. Communicate. Connect. Advocate. —fit exactly what I needed. The Chamber introduced me to great friends, connected me with business owners who could help grow the funeral home, and gave me a platform to promote my business without spending a dime on advertising.

What started as an occasional luncheon turned into committee assignments. Before I knew it, I wasn't just attending meetings—I was leading them. I became a Chamber Ambassador, then a board member, and eventually Chairman of the Board of the Grapevine Chamber of Commerce.

That put me right in the middle of some of the biggest moments in the city's modern history:

The opening of the Gaylord Texan

The launch of Cowboys Golf Club

The rise of Grapevine Mills Mall

And several major hotel developments

It was an exciting time—not just for me, but for Grapevine itself. The town was growing fast, and I was right there in the middle of it.

On par with the Chamber was Rotary. Its mission—service, integrity, and global goodwill—was admirable, but let's be honest: it was also where Grapevine's most polished professionals gathered. Attorneys, bankers, doctors, ministers, business owners. These were people who shaped the town. And as a bonus, the food was always good.

But if Rotary was polish, Ambucs was grit.

Ambucs' mission is to provide mobility and independence for people with disabilities—and this group felt like home. These were my people: guys my age who worked hard, played hard, and cared deeply about their community. Through Ambucs, I met some of my closest lifelong friends.

There was Phil "Puff Daddy" Cloud, a banker with deep Grapevine roots whose family supported just about everything in town. His last name earned him the nickname Puff; I added the "Daddy" part because that was a thing back then. He tolerated it.

Ron Stacy, whose family was famous for their "Burning Your Money" furniture commercials, ran his brother's new Grapevine store and became one of my biggest supporters and closest friends.

Mark Stanfield, a man whose polish wasn't his suit—it was his heart. Hugely successful but always looking for ways to help others.

Ronny Nordling, another banker, but more importantly, a true Grapevine insider who knew everyone and everything going on.

And then there were the Parkers, owners of Willhoite's—restaurant by day, full-blown bar by night—who knew how to mix business, community, and a good time better than anyone.

Ambucs also included City Council members, CVB leaders, and other movers and shakers. Before long, my involvement there led to something else entirely.

Golf.

Most of the Ambucs guys loved golf and charity tournaments, and eventually they pulled me into their regular Sunday morning game—the very first tee time of the day. We teed off just as the sun cracked the horizon. If I hadn't stayed in Grapevine the night before, I would have had to be up at 4:30 a.m. to make it.

It was worth every minute.

These guys didn't just become my golf buddies—they became my friends for life. They adopted a Fort Worth guy and made him a Grapevine guy. And more than anything, they promoted my business everywhere they went.

One of the things I'm most proud of came out of Ambucs: the Amtryke program. We provided adaptive bicycles and tricycles for kids with mobility challenges. These weren't just bikes; they were freedom. Kids who had never walked or ridden could suddenly ride alongside their siblings. I can still see the looks on their faces when they realized they could keep up.

Families told us how kids showed improvements in walking, communication, and confidence. The year I was Ambucs president, we attended the national meeting in Memphis and launched a bike program for injured veterans, giving them the chance to ride again with their kids. Our club gave away close to 100 bikes and trikes each year—one of the highest totals in the country.

I've had many proud moments in my career, but being an Ambuc ranks right at the top.

As I became more involved, I expanded beyond Grapevine—joining chambers in Southlake, Colleyville, Mid-Cities, and Northeast. One day, Kent Adair looked at me and said, "Martin, if you're not careful, you're going to become a country undertaker."

I laughed and said, "Kent, if I don't become a country undertaker, I'm going to go broke."

And that's exactly what I became.

Not just a funeral director—but Grapevine's funeral director.

I wasn't just in the community anymore.

I was part of it.

And that made all the difference.

Chapter 38: Docking Dilemmas

When I married Janice, I moved into her charming cottage-style home near TCU. Janice loved that house—every quirky inch of it. From the hundred-year-old pecan tree in the front yard (probably one of the largest in Fort Worth) to the equally ancient walnut tree out back, the place had more character than a full season of HGTV home makeover shows.

The one thing she didn't love.

The idea of moving to Grapevine.

We talked about it more times than I care to admit, but the answer was always a hard no. Looking back, I'm glad we stayed put. But staying in Fort Worth meant I was commuting to Grapevine every single day—and at the time, that drive felt like an endurance event designed by the people who created American Ninja Warrior.

Every road between Fort Worth and Grapevine was under construction. Lanes closed. Detours led to more detours. An hour on a good day. Two hours on a bad one. After a few months of that daily traffic purgatory, I realized I needed a backup plan.

When I first renovated the Dorris House, I had big plans for the third floor. It was going to be my personal office and a bedroom for those nights when the thought of that drive home was just too much.

That plan worked great—right up until the fire marshal showed up.

"You can't use the third floor of a commercial building for residential space unless it has a separate fire escape," he said.

That was news to me.

But this fire marshal also happened to be a Grapevine Ambuc. He paused, gave me a knowing look, and said, "Just call it storage."

Who was I to argue?

So, the third floor became my "storage" area. I stored a desk and chairs—perfect for work items. A bed and dresser—excellent for organizing old clothes. Paintings went neatly on the walls, because artwork needs proper storage, too. Everything was very tidy. I take my storage solutions seriously.

Later, when I moved to the funeral home behind the hospital, I got lucky—the building came with a nightman's apartment. It doubled as my office and a place to crash when I needed it.

But when I moved again—this time to the Main Street funeral home, the oldest in town—that luxury disappeared. The second-floor restrooms had long been removed, and with road construction still turning my commute into a slow-motion hostage situation, I needed another plan.

That's when I had what I thought was a brilliant idea.

I bought a Carver aft-cabin cruiser from a guy on Lake Texoma and had it moved to a marina on Lake Grapevine. Just like that, I had a home away from home.

I named the boat Diggit.

Diggit had everything: two bedrooms, a kitchen with a dining area, a roomy salon with a couch and big-screen TV, and a back deck perfect for morning coffee and evening drinks. I have never slept better in my life than I did on that boat.

You know the old saying about boat ownership—that the two happiest days are the day you buy it and the day you sell it?

Not me.

I loved that boat.

Living on it was the easy part.

Docking it was another story.

Diggit had two big engines, and steering was mostly done with throttle control—especially when backing into the dock. Some days, I nailed it like I'd been doing it my whole life. Other days, not so much.

The regulars at the marina quickly figured out my arrival could be entertainment.

"Oh boy," I'd hear. "Here comes Digger. Grab a beer—this should be good."

Jon, on the other hand, was a natural. Maybe it was all those video games, but he could maneuver that boat like he was playing Grand Theft Auto: Marina Edition. He made it look effortless. I made it look like a slow-motion accident.

One day, my dear friend Steve Stinson called me. Steve was battling stage-four cancer, but if you didn't know it, you'd never guess. He was tough, funny, and stubborn in the best ways.

He asked if I knew anyone selling a boat like mine. Steve and his wife Nikki had always dreamed of retiring on a lake, but they knew that dream might not come on the schedule they'd hoped.

At first, I told him I didn't know of anyone.

Then it hit me.

Everything is for sale.

Steve was one of those guys who never lost his sense of humor. At our Ambuc meetings, we had a sergeant-at-arms whose job was to fine members for just about anything—making the news, doing something dumb, or wearing something questionable in public.

One day, he stopped the meeting and told Steve to stand up.

"I've seen a lot," he said, "but I have NEVER seen this. You, my friend, are wearing a fanny pack."

Steve didn't miss a beat.

He pointed to it and said, "You mean my chemo pump?"

The sergeant-at-arms fined himself on the spot.

That was Steve.

He even played golf with that chemo pump and still hit a pitching wedge 160 yards and drove the ball 300 yards over the corner on Hole 5 at Mockingbird.

A fanny pack? Please.

That night, Steve and Nikki came out for a sunset cruise on Diggit and fell in love with the boat. The next night, they brought Steve's mom along.

When Steve asked what I wanted for it, I named a price I didn't think he'd take.

Before I could blink, his mom pulled out a check and handed it to me.

Just like that, Diggit was gone.

It was bittersweet—but I knew it was right.

Steve told me later that after his brutal chemo treatments, being on that boat was the only thing that brought him peace. For his last year, he and Nikki lived their dream—on the water.

And if that boat gave him even a little comfort during that time, then it did exactly what it was meant to do.

I think about that often, and I will never forget Steve.

Chapter 39: Chapel Charades: From Dream to Dollhouse to Desperation

Year after year, Martin Thompson Funeral Home kept growing. The Dorris House was charming, historic, and full of character—but it was also starting to feel like a shoebox.

Every available space was being used. The small carriage house in the back doubled as our chapel, and on busy services, visitations spilled into areas never meant to hold people. Families were gracious about it, but I knew the truth.

We had outgrown the house.

What I needed was a real chapel.

My plan was simple: build a new, larger chapel beside the Dorris House. I wanted it to look like it had always been there—architecturally consistent, respectful of the history, and worthy of the families we served. To do it right, I hired an architect who specialized in preserving some of Tarrant County's oldest buildings.

The design was beautiful.

Because the Dorris House sat in Grapevine's historic district, the project had to go before the Historic Commission before it could ever reach the City Council. No problem, I thought. We were thoughtful. Respectful. Careful.

At the first meeting, everything went smoothly.

"Looks great."

"This will complement the house beautifully."

"Come back next month with more detailed drawings."

Music to my ears.

Feeling confident, I gave the architect the green light to proceed with the full plans.

Then came the second meeting.

That same day, I had the chance to play a very exclusive golf course. The choice was simple: play golf or wrestle with a historic commission.

Golf won.

I finished most of the round, skipped the last couple of holes, and walked into the meeting just as my architect wrapped up his presentation. Heads were nodding again—always a good sign.

Then the questions started.

One member leaned forward.

"You know, the Dorris House is one of our most historic homes in Grapevine. I think the chapel should be shorter—not taller—than the house."

Okay. Fine. We can lower the roofline.

Another chimed in.

"And it shouldn't come all the way to the front of the house. Pull it back a few feet."

Sure. We can do that.

A third added,

"I think it should be narrower. Not so wide."

Now we were getting tight, but all right.

Then the fourth member spoke.

"I don't think it should be connected to the Dorris House at all."

Wait... what?

In a matter of minutes, my grand chapel had been reduced to something shorter, thinner, pushed back, pulled in, and awkwardly detached. What had started as a proper chapel was now beginning to resemble a Victorian dollhouse.

I finally spoke up.

"I really need a chapel," I said. "Not a dollhouse."

That's when someone offered the solution.

"Why don't you just tear down the carriage house and put the chapel there?"

That wasn't remotely what I wanted.

At this point, we were getting nowhere. So, in a last-ditch effort, I loaded up the entire Historic Commission—yes, the whole group—along with my architect and took them to Dallas. We walked Ross Avenue, looking at carriage houses behind historic homes, hoping real-world examples would help them see what I was trying to do.

They saw something.

What they saw, apparently, was a barn.

They handed me a crude elevation of what they thought would be appropriate: wooden, rustic, and completely out of place. It looked more like it belonged on a ranch than behind one of Grapevine's most historic homes—or attached to a funeral home.

By then, I had spent a great deal of money, an even greater amount of time, and somehow ended up right back where I started.

That's when it finally sank in.

I wasn't going to win this fight.

And if I wanted to keep growing, if I wanted to serve families the way they deserved—I was going to have to do the unthinkable.

I had to move.

The only question left was… where?

Chapter 40: When Growth Looked Like the Answer

After the Historic Commission effectively torpedoed my plans to build a real chapel next to the Dorris House, I knew something had to change.

As much as I loved that location—and I truly did—we were bursting at the seams. Every square foot was spoken for. Every workaround had become permanent. And there was no elegant way to grow there anymore.

At the same time, my world had expanded well beyond Grapevine.

I wasn't just involved locally anymore. I was deeply involved in the surrounding communities and the Texas Funeral Directors Association, serving on the convention committee for the following year. That meant meetings, travel, and—like all good funeral meetings—golf in the afternoon and conversations that continued long after dinner.

One of those meetings took us to Austin.

The day followed a familiar rhythm: morning meetings, afternoon golf, dinner… and then the inevitable migration to the hotel bar. That's where the real conversations always happen.

That night, a man I knew well—someone who had been a close friend of my brother's—walked up to me. We hadn't talked in years, but we picked up as if no time had passed.

His family had once owned several funeral homes in the area, selling them years earlier to a large corporate chain. He was still working for that corporation, but it was obvious he missed the funeral side of the business.

He told me something that caught my attention.

He was a close friend of the corporation's founder. Close enough, he said, that they would sell us some of their freestanding funeral homes in the Dallas–Fort Worth area.

There was one condition.

He wanted back in—and he wanted in as a partner.

I would retain 60 percent ownership. He would have 40. We would start with:

The 100-year-old Grapevine location

A Fort Worth location tied to his family's history—still being managed by his mother.

And the Hurst location, which he openly called his pride and joy

I told him I needed time to think.

When I talked to Janice, she said something simple and very honest:

"You already know you need a new Grapevine location. Expanding might solve that."

At the same time, other pieces were already in motion.

I was in the middle of buying a church in Keller—friends who were building a new church and moving out. The plan was to convert it into Keller's first funeral home. I already had a strong following there. It made sense.

And during all of this, I was also negotiating the purchase of the only funeral home in Mansfield, housed in a beautiful old mansion. The deal came together cleanly.

Within months, everything moved fast.

We relocated the Grapevine operation.

We acquired Fort Worth and Hurst.

We closed on Mansfield.

Renovations started everywhere

Business was strong. Momentum was real.

My son, who had already been working with me for years, was fully involved. My partner brought his two sons in as well.

Within months, everything was moving at once.

Grapevine finally had the space it needed. Mansfield was thriving. Fort Worth and Hurst were coming back to life. Renovations were underway, staff were in place, and for the first time, the footprint matched the vision.

My son was fully involved. His sons were coming in, too. It felt like the beginning of something generational — not just growth, but legacy.

For the first time in a long time, I wasn't scrambling. I was building.

And it felt right.

Chapter 41: Keller Didn't Want a Funeral Home (Until It Did)

At the same time, I was fighting the historic commission in Grapevine, another opportunity was unfolding just down the road in Keller—and on the surface, it made perfect sense.

I already had a steady following there. Families I served in Grapevine were coming from Keller anyway. When I learned that a church I knew well was building a new facility and planned to sell its old one, the idea was obvious: buy the building, convert it, and open Keller's first funeral home.

Simple, right?

Well, Keller had other ideas.

To open a funeral home, the city required a Specific Use Permit, which meant a formal presentation before the city council. We put together thoughtful plans, showed respect for the neighborhood, and walked in expecting a reasonable discussion.

What we got instead was a hard no.

One council member looked me straight in the eye and said,

"A funeral home just doesn't fit the vibe of an old Texas town."

I nearly fell out of my chair.

Doesn't fit the vibe?

Has this man ever watched a Western? The undertaker was always one of the first buildings in town, usually right after the saloon and before the jail. Coffins were ready before the first shootout.

But there it was. Denied.

We could appeal, but it would take ninety days. And I wasn't about to sit on my hands.

So, I went to work the only way I know how.

I walked Old Town Keller. Door to door. I introduced myself to business owners, explained what we were trying to do, and listened to their concerns. I handed out letters of recommendation from Grapevine—letters written by people who had once said they didn't need another funeral home either.

I joined the Keller Chamber. I showed up. I shook hands. I did what I'd done before, because I knew it worked.

On the night of the appeal, I told the council a simple truth.

"Keller wants great schools. Doctors. Restaurants. Libraries. Neighborhoods. Everything that makes a town great," I said. "But when a family loses someone they love, they have to leave town to celebrate that life."

That landed.

That night, Keller approved the permit.

We became Keller's first funeral home—not because of politics or pressure, but because people understood the need.

It was another reminder that persistence still mattered, that handshakes still meant something, and that sometimes common sense could still win.

And as Keller was coming together, it felt like momentum was finally lining up across the board.

Which made what came next even more unexpected.

Chapter 42: The Slow Discovery of the Trap

The call came out of nowhere.

"It's time to hit the lick log."

I had no idea what he was talking about.

He explained that we were short $80,000—not just for payroll, but for basic operating expenses.

That made no sense.

We were doing well everywhere:

Grapevine

Mansfield

Fort Worth

Hurst

And Keller was taking off.

There was no logical reason we should be short.

My mistake, the one that still makes me shake my head, was trust.

I had allowed him to keep the books.

The checks.

The bill paying.

The financial controls.

I asked for everything:

Bank statements

Balance sheets

General ledger

He promised. Then delayed. Then promised again.

Eventually, my son and I drove to the Hurst location and demanded to see the records.

His response?

He called the police and tried to have us removed for trespassing.

When the officers realized I was the majority owner, they didn't remove us—but that was the moment I knew something was very wrong.

The fight was on.

When the financial records finally arrived, they came in a box—literally dumped together. No order. No explanation.

It took me three full days to sort through them.

That's when the pattern appeared.

It started small.

A few hundred dollars one month.

A little more next.

Then more.

And more.

He—and his sons—were using the company account like a personal checking account.

By the time I finished, the total was several hundred thousand dollars.

That's why we were short.

I hired an attorney, which only deepened the hole. At the same time, we had borrowed heavily for the acquisitions—loans that Janice and I had personally guaranteed with everything we had.

That's when my banker sat me down.

He told me two things I'll never forget.

First:

If this lawsuit went to court, the bank could call the note.

Second—and worse:

In all the deals, only Janice and I had posted collateral.

My partner hadn't.

If the bank called the note, we would be wiped out.

The bank was headquartered in Weatherford, and he told me point-blank that if it went to court, they would call it.

He also told me he couldn't tell my partner that—because it would give him nothing to lose and no reason to settle.

That was never supposed to be the deal.

And in the middle of all of this, I opened the newspaper one morning and learned that I had apparently purchased a funeral home down the street from my father's.

A funeral home I never bought.

That's when I learned my name had been forged.

After a sixteen-hour mediation, I sold my interest in everything for pennies on the dollar.

Not because I wanted to.

Because the alternative was losing everything.

For the second time in my life, I walked away with nothing but my reputation, my family, and the hard lesson that trust—once broken—can cost more than money.

Chapter 43: A Profitable Partnership and a Pricey Problem

After everything that had just happened, packing it in was never an option.

My family was counting on me, Janice, Jon, and now his family. Failure wasn't some abstract concept. It had faces. And I wasn't about to let them down.

In the fire sale that followed the collapse of my previous venture, I managed to walk away with one small but powerful gift: no non-compete clause. No restrictions. No handcuffs. No invisible fence telling me where I could and couldn't go.

So, the question wasn't if I'd start again.

It was where.

The answer was easy.

Grapevine.

Around that time, I'd struck up a friendship with the president of the western division of Stewart Enterprises, a large publicly traded funeral corporation. Stewart owned Foust Funeral Home, the oldest funeral home in Grapevine, housed in another beautiful historic home on Main Street.

The problem was that Foust was barely breathing.

Less than a hundred calls a year. A location runs more on obligation than on intention. Stewart didn't quite know what to do with it—but they didn't want to close it either.

I did what I've always done.

I pitched a plan.

I drove to Dallas and sat down with the president and his regional vice president and laid it out plainly:

I would take over Foust as manager.

I would work for the bare minimum salary.

And instead of a big paycheck, I wanted a percentage of the gross profits.

They looked at me like I'd lost my mind.

"You realize this place isn't making any gross profits," one of them said.

Exactly, I told them.

No risk for you.

If I fail, you lose nothing.

If I succeed, you make money where you weren't before.

After some back-and-forth, they agreed—on one condition. I could run the funeral home my way… as long as I didn't stray too far from Stewart's playbook.

It wasn't perfect.

But it was a shot.

That Monday morning, Jon and I walked into Foust, and it felt like stepping into a time capsule—one that hadn't been opened in years. It was a beautiful late-1800s colonial mansion, but it was tired. Neglected. Quiet in a way that didn't feel peaceful.

Still, I was back in the game.

And just like when I opened Martin Thompson Funeral Home years earlier, nobody knew it yet.

I went to work.

I called on every pastor I knew. I talked about Foust at Chamber meetings, Rotary, Ambucs—anywhere someone would listen. And the beauty of Foust was its location. Right in the heart of downtown Grapevine.

Spring brought the Main Street Festival.

Fall brought Grapefest.

There were parades, homecoming, and something called Butterfly Flutterbye, which I'm still not entirely sure I understand.

I walked to meetings. Set up booths at festivals. On Halloween, we decorated the front of the house and handed out candy to kids. We weren't hiding behind a sign—we were part of Main Street again.

Stewart eventually gave me a modest budget to spruce up the place. I spent carefully. Every dime came out of gross profits. And slowly, something changed.

By the end of the first year, we had more than doubled the calls—and for the first time in years, Foust made money.

Years two, three, and four were even better. Calls increased. Profits grew. The once-forgotten funeral home was suddenly thriving.

And that's when corporate noticed.

The problem wasn't performance.

The problem was visibility.

A funeral home manager in Grapevine was making more money than some senior vice presidents. Questions started coming from New Orleans. Whispers followed.

One day, my senior vice president walked into my office—and didn't leave. To his credit, we worked well together. We brainstormed. We talked strategy. We talked about how Stewart could do better—not just financially, but for the families we served.

Then came the shake-up.

My biggest ally—the president of the western division—was promoted to the sales division and moved out of funeral operations. My regional manager fought for me, reminding anyone who would listen that Stewart was making more money because of what we'd built in Grapevine.

It didn't matter.

One by one, the people who understood the situation disappeared.

Then I was called in and told, calmly and professionally, that the agreement could no longer be honored.

Translation:

You're making too much money, and we're uncomfortable with that.

The tone changed. The friendliness faded. The lower managers grew cold.

After thirty-six years in business, after turning something dying into something profitable—I wasn't about to step backward.

So once again, I did what I've done more times than I ever expected.

I started over.

Again.

Chapter 44: Back to Basics: Fort Worth or Bust

By 2012, you'd think I'd seen just about everything this business could throw at a person.

I learned from one of the best—my dad. I built my own funeral home from scratch. I'd partnered up, gotten burned, rebuilt, and even dipped a toe into the corporate world—where I somehow managed to make them more money than they knew what to do with.

And yet, if there's one thing this business teaches you, it's this:

Just when you think you've got it figured out, life throws you a curveball.

Or, in my case… a casket on wheels.

After everything I'd been through, I felt a pull back to where it all started. Back to Fort Worth. Back to familiar streets, familiar families, and a way of doing things that made sense to me.

This time, there would be no partners.

No corporate playbooks.

No smoke and mirrors.

Just service. Done right.

That's how Martin Thompson & Son Funeral Home was born.

The idea was simple: blend old-school service with new-school value.

The industry was changing fast. Cremation had grown to more than half of all services, and many traditional funeral homes either ignored it or fought and lost business because of it. The ones who embraced cremation often went the other direction, charging families outrageous prices for very simple services.

On the opposite end were the pop-up discount funeral homes—operating out of warehouses, strip centers, or sometimes without a real facility at all. They were cheap, sure. But service was thin, rushed, and impersonal.

I saw the gap.

Families wanted affordability and dignity. Transparency and compassion. They wanted to feel cared for—not processed.

So, I went looking for a location.

What I found was a modest, well-kept building on the south side of Fort Worth. Nothing fancy. But if you squinted a little—and had some imagination—it was exactly what I needed.

Because I had no idea how the community would respond, my family pitched in. Jon went to work at Thompson's Harveson & Cole to help steady things financially while I became a one-man operation.

And when I say one man, I mean everything.

I made the calls.

I took the calls.

I met with families.

I planned services.

I filled out death certificates, printed programs, and ordered prayer cards.

I cleaned the building.

I mowed the yard.

I was on call seven days a week. From open to close. At every visitation. Every service.

You get the picture.

This time, I expanded my outreach beyond pastors and churches. I focused heavily on hospice groups—meeting nurses, social workers, and care teams who were on the front lines with families every day. I knocked on doors. I explained what we were trying to build. And I listened.

Then I did the one thing my dad always taught me mattered most.

I took care of families.

We kept prices lean and transparent. Service never slipped. No matter how simple the service—or how modest the budget—families were treated with the same respect and attention as if they were planning the most elaborate funeral in town.

Sure, I still found time to play a little golf.

Let's be honest—some of the best business conversations in Fort Worth happen between the first tee and the turn.

Slowly, momentum built.

Within a year, I brought Jon on full-time. A year later, we added two employees. Then two more. And by 2020, that one-man operation had grown to nearly five hundred calls a year.

From scratch.

In a changing industry.

In a crowded market.

After starting over more times than I ever planned to.

But this time, it was different.

This wasn't recovery.

It was confirmation.

And for the first time in a long while, it felt less like survival—and more like a well-earned victory lap.

Chapter 45: From Typewriters to Tech Titans

By 2012, running a funeral home wasn't just different from 1976; it was a different universe.

In 1976, we were living in a world of typewriters, carbon paper, and handwritten everything. By 2012, families expected websites, online obituaries, video tributes, and answers right now. And by 2026? Half the time, I feel like I need a teenage intern just to explain what button I accidentally pressed.

But here's what I've learned the hard way—starting over doesn't just mean finding a building and hanging a sign.

It means learning a new era.

And I've started over enough times to watch the entire business reinvent itself right in front of me.

1976: The Golf-Ball Typewriter Era

When I first walked into Thompson's Harveson & Cole in 1976, funeral service was about as old-school as it gets.

We typed everything—death certificates, prayer cards, guest books, letters—one keystroke at a time. When we upgraded to an electric typewriter, we thought we were living in the future.

The coolest feature wasn't spellcheck or a screen… it was that little golf-ball-looking typing element. You could swap it out, and suddenly you had a different font. Regular type, cursive—if you were feeling wild, you could get downright fancy.

My Aunt Bernadine could type faster than any human I've ever seen. In the 1970s, she hand-typed stacks of Catholic prayer cards—sometimes hundreds for one funeral—like it was nothing. She typed business letters, documents, and even my school term papers. If a keyboard had been involved, Bernadine would have won.

Then, in 1980, Vic and I finally convinced Dad to buy a computer.

That one purchase moved us from "Little House on the Prairie" to "Star Trek," at least in our minds.

When I opened Martin Thompson Funeral Home in 1998, I couldn't rely on history or a century-old name. In Fort Worth, THC didn't need to advertise; we're the advertising. Dad, Vic, Cindy, and I were out shaking hands, building trust, and letting families know who we were long before they ever needed us.

In Grapevine, nobody knew me.

So, I did what you do when you're new in town and stubborn enough to think you can pull it off:

I got louder.

Back then, marketing meant newspapers, Yellow Pages (plural—there were six), church bulletins, school directories, sports calendars, and anything else with a mailing list. I tried different angles and learned quickly what worked and what didn't.

And yes, I even did TV commercials.

My favorite one ended with me tipping my pure beaver black cowboy hat and saying, "Walk on, Sue," as our black Percheron pulled the horse-drawn hearse off-screen.

It was equal parts dignity and theater—pretty much my brand.

2012: The Year the Rules Changed (Again)

By the time I started Martin Thompson & Son in 2012, the old marketing toolbox was already disappearing.

The Yellow Pages were fading fast or really gone. Newspaper ads weren't moving the needle like they used to. Families weren't "finding you" the way they once did.

They were searching for you.

And if you weren't showing up online, you might as well have been invisible.

Websites weren't something you threw together with duct tape and hoped would work anymore. They had to be professional, fast, easy to use, and built to show up on Google. Obituaries were becoming digital. Video tributes got cleaner. Online forms and pre-planning became normal.

It wasn't enough to be good.

You had to be findable.

That's when it hit me: every time I started over, I wasn't just building a funeral home.

I was building a new version of the funeral home business.

Even the Caskets Changed

And while we're at it, people don't talk about this much, but merchandise has changed, too.

In the '80s and '90s, imported caskets had a reputation, and not a great one. But by 2012, quality improved and distribution got faster. You could order a casket the way you order a refrigerator—delivered in 24 hours—and at a fraction of the cost.

At first, I wrestled with it. I like buying American-made products. Always have.

But I've also always believed in value and fairness. If I could give a family a solid product and save them real money, that mattered. So, I did what I've always tried to do: I kept options for everybody and stayed focused on what counts most—service.

2026: The Tech Titans

Fast-forward to now, and if 2012 felt like a new world, 2024 feels like a rocket ship.

We've got SEO specialists, Google ad campaigns, Facebook and YouTube advertising, drones for property videos, and dashboards that track things I didn't even know could be tracked.

One of the biggest game-changers for us has been FDLIC. They didn't just help with marketing—they helped modernize how families interact with us.

Today, a family can plan a funeral or cremation from their couch:

Forms, selections, pricing, arrangements—right there in front of them.

In 1976, if you'd told me that would ever be normal, I'd have assumed you'd been breathing too much formaldehyde.

What Stayed the Same

But here's the part that matters—and the part I've had to remind myself of every time business changed:

Tools change.

Marketing changes.

Technology changes.

How families find you changes.

But grief doesn't.

A family still wants someone calm in the storm. Someone who tells the truth, shows up, and takes the weight off their shoulders. That part has never changed, not once—not in 1976, not in 1998, not in 2012, and not today.

The only difference is the method.

Every time I started a new funeral home, I had to adapt. And every time, I found a way.

And now—after everything I'd built, lost, rebuilt, and built again—I thought I understood change.

I didn't know it yet, but one phone call was about to remind me that no matter how much experience you have, this business can still move faster than you ever expect.

And sometimes… it moves on April Fool's Day.

Chapter 46: Funeral Moves & April Fools'

In March of 2020, I got a call from my sister that felt like the setup for the world's strangest prank.

"Cook Children's Hospital wants to buy the 8th Avenue property."

It was a strong offer — the kind you don't overthink. But there was a catch. The closing date was April 1st.

April Fool's Day.

And we had thirty days to move out.

Jon and I both knew one thing immediately: we were not letting Thompson's Harveson & Cole name disappear. But beyond that? We had no idea where we were going, how we were going to get there, or how we were going to pull this off.

And just to keep things interesting, Covid was starting to make headlines.

So now we weren't just moving a funeral home — we were doing it at the start of a pandemic.

Perfect timing.

This was the first time I'd really spent extended time inside THC since I walked out the door in 1998. Walking through those halls again felt like stepping into a time capsule. The furniture was in the same place. The pictures hung exactly where I remembered them. The casket selection room hadn't changed a bit.

At first, I was there for practical reasons — inventory, logistics, figuring out what needed to move and what didn't.

But that didn't last long.

Every room carried weight. Every chair, every table, every painting had a story attached to it. Stories of my dad. My brother. My grandparents. My aunts. Friends and coworkers who had passed through those doors and left their mark.

I made sure no one saw me linger too long.

But I was grieving.

Not just for what had been — but for what might have been.

It was bittersweet in a way that's hard to explain unless you've lived it.

Then reality set back in.

We had thirty days to find a new location, move seventy years' worth of history, renovate, and get licensed — all while the world was starting to shut down.

No pressure.

A few years earlier, I had looked at a closed church. At the time, I thought it was too big for what I needed. Wrong neighborhood. Wrong moment.

But now?

It checked every box.

A beautiful chapel.

Plenty of parking.

Good bones.

Room to grow.

I called Grace Presbytery in Dallas, which owned the building.

She asked, "When would you like to come look at it?"

I said, "I don't want to look at it. I want to know when I can get it."

Turns out Ridglea Presbyterian was using the building temporarily while their own church was being remodeled — and they were moving out on April 30th.

That night, I had moving vans lined up in the parking lot.

As awful as Covid was, it gave us one unexpected gift: time. With funerals limited to ten people and many families postponing services, we were able to renovate without disrupting operations. Inside and out, we made the space our own.

And somewhere in the middle of all that chaos, it hit me.

I worked at Thompson's Harveson & Cole for twenty-two years.

I left and built my own funeral homes for another twenty-two years.

And now — somehow — I was back.

This time, not as a kid learning the business.

This time, in charge.

God thing? Absolutely.

April Fool's joke?

Maybe just a little.

One thing I've learned for sure: if you stay in this business long enough, God will keep you humble — and occasionally laugh with you… Or at you.

Either way, you'd better be ready to move.

Chapter 47: Renovation Odyssey

When the opportunity to buy Thompson's Harveson & Cole came up, Jon and I hit the ground running, trying to find the right location — not just any location.

We looked everywhere.

South Main.

Camp Bowie.

Magnolia.

Hulen.

The 7th Street district.

And every place we found had the same problems: too small, no parking, or a renovation price tag so high it would eventually land where it always does.

On the families.

That's when we circled back to a place we already knew — John Knox Presbyterian Church.

It had been sitting empty for nearly five years, collecting dust and memories, but when we walked into it again with fresh eyes, we didn't see decay.

We saw a possibility.

The property had four main components, each with its own personality — and its own problems.

The chapel was massive and built entirely of stone. Beautiful bones, but they hadn't seen real care in decades.

The education building was constructed of what we call clinker brick — or what others might call "the drunken bricklayer style." Full of character but not forgiving.

The fellowship hall looked like it hadn't been updated since bell-bottoms were still considered a good idea.

And the parking lot? Let's just say sealcoating was not high on the priority list for a long time.

At first glance, it was a diamond in the rough — heavy emphasis on rough.

But I've learned over the years that you don't judge a building by its dust.

You judge it by its bones.

First Impressions Matter

We started outside.

Trees that had spent years staging a slow takeover were trimmed back. A new roof went on. Gutters followed. That old metal carport had to go — immediately — along with rotted cedar shake siding that belonged in another climate and another century.

We replaced it all with a stone veneer that matched the chapel perfectly.

Fresh paint on the trim. Screens on the windows. The parking lot finally got sealcoated. We moved the iron fence over from 8th Avenue, added flagpoles, pressure-washed every inch of stone and brick, and turned a jungle of a courtyard into a clean, welcoming space with artificial turf, new fencing, and a covered carport for our vehicles.

By the time we stepped back, the exterior didn't look renovated.

It looked reborn.

The Chapel Gets Its Dignity Back

The chapel was next.

You could feel its potential the moment you walked in — but it needed help.

The faded red carpet was gone.

The yellow laminate pews followed it out.

Walls that hadn't seen fresh paint since Reagan got a much-needed facelift.

We installed dark walnut hardwood floors and had custom pews built to match. The back wall — which had been hiding broken speakers behind fabric — was rebuilt properly with textured sheetrock. New lighting went in on the platform to create a warm, peaceful atmosphere.

And the stained glass.

Those beautiful windows had been hidden behind yellowed plexiglass for years. My cousin Shannon Reeves and his son replaced it with double-walled glass, finally letting the light do what it was meant to do.

When we finished, the chapel was more than twice the size of our old 8th Avenue location — and not even comparable in beauty.

Offices, Classrooms, and Reality

The education wing and offices were straightforward by comparison.

New flooring.

Fresh paint.

Updated bathrooms.

And the office furniture from 8th Avenue? It somehow looked even better in its new home.

Sometimes simple changes make the biggest difference.

The Fellowship Hall (a.k.a. The Biggest Problem)

Then there was the fellowship hall.

The bathrooms made gas station restrooms look like luxury accommodations. The drop ceiling barely reached nine feet — and that was generous — with missing tiles and lighting that did no favors. The kitchen was a place I wouldn't have trusted with a sandwich. The walls were wrapped in dark pine paneling that soaked up light and joy equally.

So, we did what needed to be done.

We ripped it all out.

Once the drop ceiling was gone, we discovered twelve- to fifteen-foot ceilings hiding above it — a gift we didn't expect. We insulated, drywalled, textured, and painted everything. Added a second air conditioner, because Texas summers don't negotiate. The kitchen was gutted and rebuilt, with new catering equipment installed.

Janice and I found a tile floor so good it stopped us both in our tracks.

Built-in speakers went in. Large screens on each end for video tributes. And when it was finished, I gave it a name to honor where we came from.

The Drawing Room.

It was finally a space I was proud to bring families into.

The People Who Made It Possible

None of this happens without the right people.

Luis Prieto and his wife, Martha Cabrera, worked tirelessly to bring this place to life. Their craftsmanship was exceptional, but more than that, they cared. Along the way, they became friends — and their work continues to be part of what we do today.

And thanks to Covid — one of the few silver linings in that season — we were able to complete the entire renovation without disrupting services.

Looking back, what started as a forgotten church became a beautiful, functional funeral home — one built with intention, restraint, and respect for the families who would walk through its doors.

Once again, I was reminded:

Sometimes the right place isn't the one you find first.

It's the one you come back to — when you're finally ready to see it.

Chapter 48: Funeral Service in Pandemic Times

When I first started in the funeral business, dangerous diseases existed, but nothing truly shook our profession—until AIDS hit in the mid-1980s.

Back then, we didn't know what we know now. We didn't have today's training, today's protocols, or today's equipment. What we had was a whole lot of unknown... and a whole lot of fear—especially in the embalming room.

The first AIDS case we handled at Thompson's Harveson & Cole became a moment I'll never forget. Dad called my brother, Vic, and me into his office and said, "How can we ask our employees to do something we aren't willing to do ourselves?"

So, Vic and I made the call and did the embalming.

Our "protective equipment" was what you'd call early-American improvisation: two pairs of gloves—each with a few too many holes—and thin hospital gowns that didn't cover nearly as much as they should have. No face shields. No modern PPE. Just two brothers trying to do the job right.

I remember that day vividly because I was wearing my favorite custom-made suit. When we finished, Vic looked at my pants and said, "What's that spot?"

I looked down, and my heart dropped.

In that moment, my brain didn't do logic. It panicked. I threw that suit away in a biohazard bag and drove home wearing nothing but a hospital gown. Looking back, I know it was an overreaction. But at the time, with what we didn't know, it felt like survival.

AIDS was terrifying in those early years—but in sheer volume, nothing compared to Covid-19.

When Covid hit in early 2020, Fort Worth didn't feel it immediately. We watched New York and other major cities get overwhelmed and thought, this is awful… but it's far away.

Then the calls started coming in.

And what I saw wasn't just grief. It was a different kind of grief—grief mixed with shock, guilt, and helplessness.

Families would sit across from me and say some version of the same thing: "We weren't allowed to be there." Weeks… sometimes months… separated from their loved ones. No hand to hold. No bedside goodbye. No last conversation. And then, even after death, they couldn't gather the way families are meant to gather.

I have been in the funeral service nearly my entire life, and I've never seen anything like that. It wasn't just heart-wrenching.

It was cruel.

By the fall of 2020, Martin Thompson & Son and Thompson's Harveson & Cole were busier than ever. We were handling more Covid deaths than I care to count. We adjusted constantly—capacity limits, distancing, sanitizing, livestreams, graveside services with 10 people standing 6 feet apart, like strangers.

We still found a way to give families something sacred.

Then one Sunday afternoon, I played golf.

Everything was fine until the last few holes—then my legs started aching. Then my back. By the time I got home, I felt awful, and the next morning I knew something was wrong.

I found the first available Covid test and drove over. The line of cars wrapped around like it was the latest iPhone release—two and a half hours for a drive-thru nose swab.

Finally, it was my turn. The nurse swabbed me, disappeared, and returned a few minutes later.

She leaned into the window and said, "You're positive."

I pulled into an empty parking lot and just sat there, staring straight ahead.

I had buried too many people who died from Covid not to think the thought that came next: Am I next?

I couldn't go home—Janice's mother lives with us and was at high risk. So, I booked a hotel room on my phone—one where I could do everything digitally and avoid contact—then I called Janice.

Of course, she said she was coming home immediately. And of course, I told her no. I told her I was already in the hotel. I asked her to pack a bag, put it in her trunk, and when she got home, I'd swing by masked and gloved and grab it without getting close.

I made it through.

But too many didn't.

Including one of my best friends, Phil "Puff Daddy" Cloud. Phil was one of the first people to welcome me to Grapevine. He was my golf buddy, my Ambucs brother, and one of the best people I've ever known.

One day, he was here.

And then he wasn't.

Even now, I miss him.

COVID changed funeral service overnight. Viewings were limited. Funerals went virtual. Families grieved alone. We had to learn new ways to do the oldest work in the world.

But it also reminded me of something I already knew deep down:

When everything else gets stripped away, families still need dignity. They still need compassion. And they still need somebody steady to help carry the weight.

That's what we've always tried to be.

Through AIDS. Through Covid. Through whatever comes next.

Chapter 49: Nobody Does This Alone

As I sit here today, looking back at where we've been and forward to where we're headed, one thing is crystal clear: no funeral home succeeds because of one person. Not the owner. Not the name on the sign. Not even the guy who's been around the longest.

Funeral homes thrive—or fail—because of their people.

And I've been blessed with some of the very best.

A couple of years ago, my son Jon had an idea. He suggested we throw our hat into the ring for the Star-Telegram's DFW Favorites Awards. It used to be called Readers' Choice, and it gave families we've served, along with friends and community members, a chance to vote for the funeral homes they trust most.

I'll admit, I didn't give it much thought. Awards come and go.

Then the results came in.

Thompson's Harveson & Cole took home Silver.

Martin Thompson & Son won Gold.

After 113 years in business, Thompson's Harveson & Cole was finally recognized—and my son, in just twelve years, finished first.

Not bad, Son. Not bad at all.

The following year, Thompson's Harveson & Cole took home Gold, and Martin Thompson & Son won Silver. We can share.

The Backbone at Thompson's Harveson & Cole

At THC, I've been fortunate to keep two men who represent the very best of funeral service.

Roger Kersten is a workhorse in every sense of the word. He's been with us for over forty years, and I honestly don't know how the place would run without him. Roger wears more hats than a department store mannequin during a clearance sale. He meets families, works funerals, solves problems before they become problems—and somehow still finds time to do things most people wouldn't even attempt.

He is, without question, the best cosmetologist I've ever worked with, thanks in no small part to my dad's old-school training and Roger's willingness to master it. And if that weren't enough, he breeds birds and maintains aviaries at two different homes. I'm convinced Roger doesn't know the meaning of the word "no." Families love him, and so do we.

Then there's Charles Surber, a man I've known since my Boy Scout days. He was an Eagle Scout with Troop 32 when I first joined, and by the time I reached Nolan, he was finishing his final year. Years later, I even bought furniture from his store before he closed it and came to work with us.

Charles is the definition of a gentleman. Impeccably dressed. Calm. Steady. Reassuring. Having lost his wife to COVID, Charles brings a depth of compassion that can't be taught—only lived. Families feel that, and they trust him because of it. Charles just officially retired, kind of, maybe, he still pops in and helps when needed.

In the office, I'm lucky to work alongside my twin sister, Martha. We share a sense of humor that's probably best described as twisted, but I chalk that up to the twin thing. We've been laughing—and surviving—together our entire lives.

And then there's Luis Prieto and his wife, Martha Cabrera, who keep things running smoothly at both Thompson's Harveson & Cole and Martin Thompson & Son. Quite frankly, I couldn't do this without them.

Seeing the Difference

After more than fifty years in funeral service, you develop a kind of radar. You can tell when someone is faking it—when the words sound right, but the heart isn't fully there. You see it in their posture, in how they speak, in how quickly they move on to the next task.

I've always taken pride in being a good funeral director. My dad instilled in me the belief that every family deserves care, dignity, and respect, and I've tried to live up to that every single day.

But I can say this without hesitation: I could not do what I do without Jon.

Jon has taken this calling to another level.

His care for families isn't learned behavior. It isn't scripted. It's genuine. The way he listens. The way he speaks. The way he stands with families—not in front of them, not above them, but with them—is something you can't teach.

When It Matters Most

Recently, we helped the family of a young firefighter. It was a tragic loss. He was deeply loved by his family and by the fire department he served. This happened just a few days before Christmas, and anyone who knows firefighters understands they are a true band of brothers.

Throughout that Christmas period, the fire department kept at least two firefighters with him at the funeral home, twenty-four hours a day. They didn't want him alone.

Jon personally handled everything.

He met with the family. He helped them find a church large enough for the service. He went with them to the church to make arrangements. He helped them find the best cemetery property and went with them again to handle those details. He was with them on Christmas Day, going over plans when most people were at home opening presents.

On the day of the service, the fire department showed up in full force—every fire vehicle, every uniform, every brother standing in quiet respect. It was one of those funerals you don't forget.

At the cemetery, the firefighter's wife asked Jon if he could get her children a rose to place on their father's casket.

I looked over and saw Jon on one knee, holding the roses, speaking softly to the children at eye level. He didn't just hand them a flower and move on. He met them where they were.

I don't know why that moment caught me the way it did. On the surface, it seemed small. But it wasn't.

It was instinct.

It was the look of a father with children his own age. The kind of care that comes from knowing exactly what it means to protect, to comfort, and to stand in for someone who can't be there anymore.

That's not something you learn in mortuary school.

That's who he is.

Carrying It Forward

At Martin Thompson & Son, I've stepped back and handed Jon the reins—not just a name people constantly misspell, but a funeral home built on trust. Under his leadership, it's grown so much that we had to buy the building next door just to make room. He and his team helped renovate it into a bright, open, comfortable space for families and staff alike. Next on the list is renovating the original building.

And Jon doesn't do it alone.

Peyton is what I call The Rockstar Embalmer. She's incredibly talented, works harder than anyone I know, and is so dedicated to her craft that she attends embalming conferences simply to get better. Her restorative work is nothing short of art.

David and Jason are the workhorses. They meet families, take calls, handle services, and never complain.

Bessie and Jerald have helped us reach communities we once couldn't serve, allowing us to care for more families from all walks of life.

In the office, there's Sophia—always smiling, always working, and thankfully fluent in Spanish. She helps families navigate some of the hardest moments in their own language.

And with cremation now being such a significant part of funeral service, we're fortunate to have Gary, the best crematory operator in the business. He runs it with professionalism and pride—keeping it what I like to call Channel 5 Ready.

What I'm most proud of at Martin Thompson & Son is this: families receive great care and real value without cutting corners. Every family is treated with dignity and respect—the way it should be.

So, to Jon, and to every member of both teams: thank you.

Because no matter how long you've been in this business, no matter how much experience you have, one truth never changes—

Nobody does this alone.

Chapter 50: Blood, Business, and the Funeral Home

Ah, yes — the family business.

From the outside, people imagine warm hugs, shared victories, and generations working in perfect harmony. It's more like herding cats in a thunderstorm. Family brings loyalty, history, and heart into a business — but it also brings strong opinions, stubborn streaks, and the occasional collision.

I've already talked a lot about my dad, the driving force behind Thompson's Harveson & Cole, and my brother Vic — the Crown Prince — whose charm, humor, and vision could have taken the firm even further if life had allowed it.

But the Thompson influence didn't stop there.

Before my mom ever set foot in the funeral home, she had already mastered several careers: chauffeur, cook, housekeeper, and full-time Mom. When she joined the business, she brought every bit of that discipline with her.

Back in those days, prepaid funeral funds were held in trust accounts audited regularly by the Texas Banking Commission. Everything had to balance — down to the penny. We had computers, but my mom trusted her spreadsheets. For all I know, she might've used an abacus.

The auditors were always amazed. Not a single cent ever out of place. I'm convinced they left every year wondering if my mom possessed some kind of supernatural accounting ability.

My oldest sister, Cindy, took a slightly different path at first, working in hospital dietary services before joining the funeral home full-time in the early 1980s. Back then, women weren't exactly encouraged to become licensed funeral directors — it simply wasn't the norm.

Cindy changed that.

She made the daily drive to the Dallas Institute of Funeral Service, earned her license, and after my dad passed away, she led Thompson's

Harveson & Cole with strength, grace, and determination. She proved that women not only belong in funeral service but also excel at it.

My sister Teacy also spent years working at the funeral home before earning her funeral director's license. Then she pulled a classic pivot and traded it for a real estate license. But once the family business gets into your blood, it never really leaves. She put in her time, learned the trade, and made her mark.

My brother Tim took a very different road — one that led all the way to Rome. After high school, he entered Holy Trinity Seminary at the University of Dallas, and later, the Bishop of Fort Worth sent him to the Vatican to complete his studies.

During the summers, Tim worked at the funeral home, which may have reinforced his calling, because this business has a way of sending a man straight to prayer.

When Tim was ordained a Deacon at the Vatican, our family traveled to Rome for the ceremony. We stayed near the Vatican, and Tim insisted on taking us to his favorite restaurants, which involved a lot of walking and far more fish than I ever expected.

I kept asking where the real Italian food was. Turns out, that was the real Italian food.

Despite the seafood overload, I can say without hesitation that Tim made the right choice. He loves his church, his parishes, and his people. I may be biased, but I believe he's one of the finest priests I've ever known — and as humble as they come.

And then there's my champion — my twin sister Martha.

In my book, she's Mother of the Year every single year. She raised four daughters — the "Mini Marthas" — who are all exactly like her. She's spent her life serving others, whether as a teacher, counselor, mother, or funeral home employee. Through it all, she's been my biggest supporter from the time we were toddlers to today.

Now she's back working with me at THC, and it feels right.

Running a funeral home with your family is messy. It's emotional. It's chaotic. But it's also deeply meaningful. I wouldn't trade the memories, the arguments, or the lessons for anything.

Because at the end of the day, family is what keeps this business alive.

And even when we disagree — when we argue, clash, or see things differently — when a family walks through our doors on the worst day of their lives, we stand together.

Every time.

Chapter 51: Who Really Backed the Note

Over the years—as you've probably gathered by now—I've had the opportunity (and the nerve) to start more than one funeral home. From the outside, it might look like careful planning and good timing.

The truth is, none of it would have happened without people willing to stand behind me.

The very first location of Martin Thompson Funeral Home in Grapevine didn't come together because of some brilliant business maneuver on my part. It happened because Janice's Aunt Connie, along with her parents, Myrle and Fawn—who I came to think of as my second set of parents—believed in me.

They didn't just offer encouragement or kind words over dinner. They backed me financially when it mattered most. They took a chance on an idea, on a vision, and frankly, on me.

People like to say, "It takes a village."

In my case, it took a very generous and trusting family.

As business grew, I quickly learned another lesson: vision alone doesn't keep the lights on. You need a banker who understands what you're trying to build—and who's willing to say yes when others hesitate.

That's how Bill Johnson at the Bank of Commerce in downtown Fort Worth entered the picture. Bill wasn't just a banker who nodded politely while you talked. He listened. And more importantly, when the time came, he said, "Yes."

In business, that kind of banker is worth his weight in gold. Or at the very least, he's an ace you want in your back pocket.

From there, my banking path led me to Texas Bank in Grapevine, which eventually introduced me to Phil "Puff Daddy" Cloud at Bank of the West—a name that still means a lot to many people in this community.

Phil wasn't a banker who lived behind a desk. He was a true community banker, the kind who knew your story, your risks, and your intentions. He believed in what I was trying to do, and that belief carried me through moments when the numbers alone might not have.

When Phil passed away, I was already back in Fort Worth, expanding again, buying old churches and properties along Granbury Road, dreaming a little bigger than before. With those projects came the need for a new banking relationship in Fort Worth.

And that's where golf comes in.

Here's a little free advice: if you ever want to make the right business connections, get yourself a golf course membership. Some of the best deals I've ever made didn't happen in a boardroom. They happened between tee boxes.

One day during a round, a golf buddy suggested Pinnacle Bank. That's how I met Gary Noel, who has been my banker for the past several years. Gary understands me, understands my business, and understands when to step in—and when to let things breathe.

We're both nearing the end of our careers, and I'm hopeful Gary will be my last banker.

Fingers crossed.

But if I'm being completely honest—and this is where the truth of this chapter lives—the most important person in this entire story isn't a banker, a business partner, or even me.

It's Janice.

Without her unwavering support over the past thirty-four years, none of this would have been possible. She's been my rock, my sounding board, and the person who's kept me at least somewhat sane—no small feat when you're married to a funeral director with a head full of ideas.

She's stood beside me through every risk, every expansion, every setback, and every "what was I thinking?" moment.

And let's be clear—I'm not always the easiest person to stand beside.

But she's done it anyway.

So yes, I've been fortunate to have great bankers, supportive family members, and mentors who believed in me. But when it comes down to who really backed the note—who believed when it mattered, there's only one answer.

Janice.

Chapter 52: Between Tee Times and Lifetimes

Thanks to an incredible staff and a wife who truly understands the sacred art of a well-timed tee-off, I've managed to sneak in a little more golf these days with a great group of guys over at Ridglea.

We call ourselves the Rubin Group, which sounds far more official than it is. Think of a less secret society, more social club with a mild golf addiction. Barry's crew has a game going almost every day, and I join them whenever I can—at least once a week, sometimes more if the funeral gods are feeling generous.

Most evenings, you'll find us gathered near the South Course—having a drink, trading stories, and engaging in the kind of good-natured ribbing that only men of a certain age and comfort level can get away with. You know the saying, "If you can't stand the heat, stay out of the kitchen"? Well, this kitchen runs hotter than the Ridglea men's grill.

Which, come to think of it, has actually caught fire twice in the past few years.

Coincidence? I think not.

Somewhere along the way, I've also become a domino player—at least in my own mind. The guys were kind enough to give me lessons, which mostly involved saying, "Sit down, we'll teach you," and then taking my money one hand at a time. I consider those losses tuition paid to the School of Hard Blocks.

As for my golf swing… well, it's still as unorthodox as a pink flamingo trying to ride a unicycle. But somehow, I'm playing some of the best golf of my life. And when I inevitably shank a shot, I just smile and remind myself, "At least I don't have to make a living doing this."

Looking back, I realize how fortunate I've been with friends.

It started early—with Jimmy Suarez, back in first grade. I ran into Jimmy recently, and we took a walk down memory lane. He mentioned he'd just sold his bar on West 7th, The Abbey Pub. The funny part?

Jimmy and his wife don't drink. That's like a vegan running a steakhouse—and making a fortune doing it.

Many of my Boy Scout buddies are still close friends. One of them, Phil Shaw, even married my twin sister, Martha. Talk about keeping it in the family.

Then there's Chris, who's had a tremendously successful career in the medical field, running companies all over the country. He and his wife recently built a spectacular home in the Hill Country with panoramic views so impressive that I'm convinced they're giving the Grand Canyon a run for its money.

And of course, there's Griff—my partner-in-crime for every member-member tournament I can talk him into. We try to play once a week. Griff has enjoyed a successful career in banking and lives in a great house on Eagle Mountain Lake. But why stop there when you can buy the house next door, too?

Officially, it's for his parents in case they ever need care.

Unofficially, it's the ultimate man cave.

Griff's dad passed away a few years ago, and I was honored to serve his family. He's buried at Oakwood Cemetery, overlooking downtown Fort Worth. Griff placed a golf ball on a tee at his marker, and every time I have a service there, I make sure it's still perfectly teed up.

His mother—Mrs. G—just celebrated her one hundred and second birthday and still lives independently on Eagle Mountain Lake. She's sharper than most people half her age and twice as much fun.

Then there's Clayne, or CD as we call him. He followed a girl to Michigan—a girl who could easily pass for Christie Brinkley's twin sister. Honestly, I would've followed her, too.

Clayne stayed in funeral service, and because Michigan requires a four-year degree, he went back to school and nailed it. He eventually became Chair of the Anatomical Department at the University of Michigan. Not bad for a Texas boy. Inspired by what I was doing with Martin Thompson & Son, Clayne and his family opened Fraser Family

Funeral Home just outside Detroit, offering low-cost funerals and cremation. I couldn't be prouder of him. He just told me the South Lyon Chamber awarded them Business of the Year.

My Grapevine guys—Ron Stacy and Ronny Nordling—are still constant in my life, and we play whenever schedules allow.

All in all, it's been a hell of a ride, and I'm nowhere near ready to say what I said when I graduated high school: "The party's over." Quite the opposite. I'm having too much fun to stop now.

When I started writing this project, I thought I might finally tell some of the wild stories from the funeral business. Trust me, there are plenty. Friends have been encouraging me to write them down for years.

But as I wrote, I realized some stories are better left untold—out of respect for the families who trusted me during their most private moments. I take that trust seriously, so those stories will stay buried.

I also considered diving into some of the harder chapters of my life, but let's be honest—who wants a sob story when you can have a laugh instead?

In the end, I wanted this to be a fun, quirky look at my life—with all its twists, turns, friendships, and fairways. Writing it has been as much for me as it has been for you, and I hope I haven't bored you too badly along the way.

I recently finished reading Origin, which gave me a glimpse into where we may be headed—both in life and in our profession. It's comforting to know Jon will be the one steering the ship into the future.

As for me, I'll keep working because I love what I do.

But Jon—don't expect me to be clocking in at ninety.

This time, I'm not starting over.

I'm finishing strong.

Chapter 53: Four A.M.

For years, New Year's Eve meant the same thing for Janice and me: good intentions, bad decisions, and waking up on New Year's Day feeling about as awful as a person can feel.

Like a lot of people, we thought New Year's Eve was supposed to be celebrated loudly. Expensive food. Crowded places. Anything and everything is put in front of you to drink. And every January first, I'd swear I'd never do it again.

Eventually, we decided we were done wasting money and energy on all of that.

One year, Janice and I stayed home. I went to Central Market, bought crab cakes, shrimp, and a bottle of Prosecco. By nine o'clock, I was in bed. I never saw a ball drop.

That night, I had a dream.

I've always had vivid dreams—detailed, persistent ones. And in that dream, a thought kept repeating itself:

You should write a book.

Everyone had been telling me that for years. About the stories. About the funeral business. About the things I'd seen and experienced. I'd always brushed it off.

But this time, the idea didn't fade when I woke up.

On New Year's Day, I was awake at four in the morning—bright-eyed and wide awake. I went downstairs, scrolled through Facebook for a few minutes, got bored, and the thought came back again.

Write a book.

I didn't know the first thing about writing a book. But I did know how to open Microsoft Word and start a new document. So that's what I did.

In that dream, the first stories were already there. I started writing them. Every night, more would come. Every morning around four, I'd sit down and type as fast as I could. My fingers couldn't keep up with my head.

After a few months, another dream started coming—this one quieter, but firmer.

These are not your stories to tell.

These were private moments in people's lives. Families had trusted me during their worst days. And here I was, writing about grand funerals, sad funerals, odd families, and difficult families.

The voice was right.

No matter how hard I tried to come up with the next story, that's all I could hear. Finally, I admitted it—to myself.

You're right.

I scrapped the entire thing.

By then, Word informed me I was about twenty-five thousand words in. It was disappointing, but I knew it was the right decision.

Then the dreams shifted again.

There are parts of this you can tell, they said.

The parts about you.

Growing up around funeral service. How it shaped me. How it formed my sense of humor, my values, my view of life and death. I started a new document, and this time the words came even faster.

I had to plan early: was this going to be a tell-all or something lighter?

I chose humor.

I wrote. And rewrote. And rewrote again. When I finally finished, I gave it to Janice, my mother-in-law, and a good friend who truly loves books.

Then I read it myself—for the first time.

It was awful.

It wasn't funny. It was corny. Disjointed. I was eight-year-old Martin on one page, forty-year-old Martin on the next, then back to college. It was all over the place.

So, I reorganized everything chronologically. Then I rewrote every chapter—some five times, some ten.

When I finished again, I found an editor who specialized in memoirs and sent it to her. The first big change she wanted was the title. She didn't like Digger. We went back and forth and eventually landed on Funeral Begins with Fun.

It wasn't my first choice. Honestly, it was my last.

But while she was editing, I was still waking up at four in the morning—and I needed something new to write.

That's when I wrote Talking Dog $20.

I based it on my favorite joke. I named the dog Mulligan—because golf, dogs, funeral service, my friends, and my wife pretty much sum up my life. I let him run wild. Adventures, stories, absurdity.

I loved writing that book.

When I sent it to my editor, I expected enthusiasm. Instead, I got an email a few days later:

This is a waste of time. It isn't good. It doesn't have a story.

I was devastated.

But instead of quitting, I rewrote it. When I finally found the story—one rooted deeply in my own life—the old material no longer fit. That version became Second Chances, and it came straight from the heart.

While that was being edited, I wrote Heart and Humanity, a storyteller's history of funeral service from the beginning. I finished it before edits ever started.

I don't think my editor ever really liked the dog books. But I loved the original version too much to let it die.

So, I posted a chapter a day on Facebook.

Then I realized people read posts more often if there's an image. I started creating cartoon-style images for each chapter—something I'd never done before. It was hard. Frustrating. And incredibly rewarding.

Thirty-eight chapters. Thirty-eight days. Thirty-eight images.

When it was done, I realized something else:

This really should be a book.

So, I taught myself editing. Formatting. Word's invisible gremlins. Photoshop's cruel sense of humor. ISBNs. Barcodes. Paperback and hardcover covers. IngramSpark and its endless obstacles.

Every victory was followed by another, " Are you kidding me? moment.

But the dreams kept coming. And at four in the morning, they were usually right.

Now, somehow, I've published The Mulligan Chronicles, Second Chances, Heart and Humanity, and I've come back to this one—Digger: Unearthing Life's Stories.

I don't know exactly how much of this journey belongs on these pages.

But I do know this:

For the past three years, this has been a huge part of my life.

And every bit of it started at four in the morning.

Conclusion: Burying the Last Laugh

Well, folks, here we are at the end of Unearthing Life's Stories. If you've made it this far, I'm either doing something right—or you're simply the kind of person who finishes what they start. Either way, congratulations. You've got more willpower than most people at an all-you-can-eat buffet.

As we prepare to close the lid on this book (pun absolutely intended), I hope you've found the journey as entertaining as I have. From the wild adventures of running a funeral home to the less glamorous tales of commuting, pets with strong personalities, and the occasional unexplained moment, it's been a ride filled with laughter, lessons, and maybe just a little lunacy.

And let's be honest—if you can't find humor in life's everyday absurdities, you're missing out on one of its greatest gifts.

I've shared a lot here—probably more than my family would've preferred (sorry, y'all). But that's the price they pay for having a storyteller in the family. While I may have taken a few detours, cracked a few jokes, and got sidetracked along the way, I hope you've seen the heart behind it all.

Life has a way of keeping you humble. Some days you're driving the hearse. Other days, you're the poor soul stuck behind it in rush-hour traffic. Either way, it's the stories we tell, the laughs we share, and the people we love that make the journey worthwhile.

So, what's the moral of all these tales?

It's simple: don't take life too seriously.

Whether you're dealing with a two-hour commute, a misbehaving parrot, or a funeral home renovation that feels like it'll never end, remember to laugh. Because at the end of the day, life is too short not to enjoy the ride—even if it comes with a few unexpected bumps and the occasional parking ticket.

Acknowledgments

First and foremost, to my wife, Janice, and my son, Jon—you are the foundation of everything good in my life. Your love, patience, and unwavering support made all this possible, and I am forever grateful.

I also owe a debt of gratitude to Fawn and Myrle Furry and Aunt Connie. Without your belief in me and your willingness to take a chance, this would have been possible.

To Jimmy Suarez and his dad, who introduced me to a lifelong love of golf;

To Griffin Gunter and his parents, who welcomed me into their family and helped shape my early years;

To Chris Guinn and his family, whose friendship and humor made the journey lighter;

To Clayne Fraser, my partner-in-crime, co-pilot, and source of endless stories;

And to Eddie Robinson, whose spirit and loyalty still guide me today.

To my Grapevine bunch—Phil Cloud, Ron Stacy, Ronny Nordling, and the many movers and shakers who believed in me and helped me build a dream.

To my bankers (you know who you are), the Rubin Group at Ridglea, and everyone I've ever played golf with, served as a funeral director, or shared a good laugh with—thank you for adding your own chapters to my story.

To the Catholic Church, and to the priests and nuns who served with true servant hearts—thank you for doing your best to educate a stubborn kid and instill a little religion and a lot of discipline. You made more of a difference than you know.

To the pastors and church leaders who trusted me and allowed me to serve their church families—thank you.

To the hospice workers who make the end-of-life journey gentler and more meaningful for the families we serve, and who passed along kind words when it mattered most—thank you.

To my professors at Texas Wesleyan College, especially Dr. Donnelly and Dr. Fleming—you helped me finally learn how to learn. Your patience and belief changed the course of my life.

And to my fellow funeral directors across the country who dedicate themselves to one of the most sacred and humbling callings there is—I am proud to stand among you.

Each of you, in your own way, helped build this life and this book.

I couldn't have done it without you.

Thank you—for everything.

About the Author

Martin Thompson is a lifelong funeral director, storyteller, and author based in Fort Worth, Texas. A third-generation funeral professional, he has spent nearly five decades serving families at their most vulnerable moments—work that has shaped both his perspective on life and the stories he tells.

Martin is the owner of Thompson's Harveson & Cole Funeral Home and Martin Thompson & Son Funeral Home, where compassion, tradition, and a deep respect for community guide everything he does. Over the years, he has learned that even in the face of loss, humor and humanity often rise to the surface, offering comfort when it is needed most.

He is the author of Funeral Begins with Fun; The Mulligan Chronicles: Talking Dog $29 – A Texas Tale; The Mulligan Chronicles: Second Chances – A Story of Loss, Faith and Redemption; and Heart and Humanity: A Funeral Director's Chronicle of the World's Oldest Calling. His writing blends humor, faith, and reflection, drawing from a lifetime spent listening to stories that matter.

Martin lives in Texas with his wife, Janice, and their two dogs, one of whom is convinced he is the inspiration for far more stories than he deserves. When he isn't writing, Martin enjoys golf, history, and time spent with family and friends.